Heaven by the Hems

MARINA DE BERG

Heaven by the Hems

From Stage To Cloister

Translated from the French by
JOANNA RICHARDSON

SHEED AND WARD - NEW YORK

Contents

Heaven by the Hems

I

Anxiety

I WAS an orphan, but till I was twenty-three I thought I could make a success of my life. I had always dreamt of being a dancer, an actress and a film star, and the dream had come true, I was dancing, I was acting in plays, I was taking more and more important parts. I didn't ask myself if that was real happiness. I hadn't time, I was swept along by an unceasing current. I was working hard. I was meeting all sorts of people, I was joining wholeheartedly in the wild frivolities which went with my chosen professions in Paris. When moods of depression came over me, I refused to believe that I was disillusioned. I put my black humour down to nervous exhaustion. Besides, these moments of depression never lasted long. I was determined to make a career for myself, and I felt I had the courage to overcome the obstacles that were bound to arise. In fact, I felt I was an adaptable young girl and not a heroine struggling in torment.

It was in 1950, when I was just eighteen, that something went wrong in the uneventful progress of my dream life.

After a period of intensive work, followed by a period of wild gaiety, I found myself in a state of acute depression. Instead of trying to escape from it, as I usually did, I abandoned myself to it. I had always avoided criticizing my

way of life, but now I plunged into a fury of self-criticism.
I accused myself of being capricious, unstable, superficial,
frivolous. I made a list of all the things I'd managed to
achieve. I found nothing but emptiness. I had neglected
everything essential. I had pursued only shadows. In fact, I
was busy ruining my life. I very soon decided that the way I
had chosen would never bring me what I sought: the kind
of joy my heart yearned for now that it doubted its thirst
for worldly success. In a few days I was lost once more in
the quicksands of loneliness.

Weeks went by like this. I tried to understand what was
happening to me. I was certainly having a breakdown.
That's what always happens when you live without a
minimum inner stability: you collapse completely. But I
had grown listless, and so I did nothing about it. I went on
dancing, rehearsing my parts, without looking for a remedy.
I told myself that a solution would turn up eventually, that
such conflicts between the thirst for fame and the search for
the absolute could not remain unresolved.

One evening, a friend of mine, to whom I had confided
my distress, suggested that I might join the Dominican
Tertiaries. I would not have to renounce the world if I
joined the Tertiaries, and in the Rule I should find a spiritual
basis on which I could reorganize my life.

I was delighted at the idea. It had the advantage of being
simple, of not turning things upside down. It avoided any
sharp break. Besides, the Dominicans were a modern,
up-to-date Order; people talked about them with admiration; it would be pleasant to belong to their ranks. And then,
this quest, this Dominican Rule, led finally to God, and to
the absolute.

The Dominican Tertiaries met in the Rue de la Glacière.
All I had to do was to meet the Mother Superior, and ask

her to admit me. I made my decision one morning. It was grey and damp, and I felt my enthusiasm diminish at every Métro station. I was going to meet a stiff old woman in corsets and spectacles, a black suit and grey stockings, who would read me a lecture. I would hardly be any further on. I didn't need anyone to tell me what I ought or ought not to do. I needed someone to teach me how to want to do the right thing.

The meeting was held in a room on the second floor. There were crowds of people there, older women and young girls, too, laughing and talking eagerly. I found the Mother Superior. She was elegant, and her eyes shone with goodness and intelligence. I went up to her. I had nearly forgotten my distress and I had lost the temptation to smile.

'Madame,' I said to her, without beating about the bush, 'I want to join the Dominican Tertiaries.'

It was she who smiled.

'What's your occupation?'

'Classical dancing, and acting.'

I expected her to be surprised. People usually imagine that religion and dancing do not go together. She was not surprised.

'You shouldn't have much time,' she answered, 'if you take your profession seriously. Our Rule binds us to daily Mass, to fifteen minutes' prayer with the rosary. You look rather delicate to me. Perhaps it wouldn't be wise to take this time from your rest. But I have no right to discourage you. Go and listen to Father H., who has come from Nancy to preach at our annual retreat. You'll like him. He is a mystic and a saint.'

Father H. preached in a little chapel. All the available space was filled with benches. It was dark. You saw nothing but faces, all turned towards this ascetically thin priest, who spoke almost in a whisper, as if he was telling a secret. He told us how all the joy and watchful affection that fill our childhood and vanish with maturity could be found again in devotion to Our Lady. He told us how man's loneliness on earth could be alleviated by looking up to Heaven.

I came out overwhelmed. I had drunk in all Father H.'s words. I was sure that he was not deceived, and was not deceiving us. The absolute that I blindly sought in this earthly world would be found, instead, in the direction of heaven. There were the keys to all true happiness.

I followed the retreat with passionate interest. I stopped thinking I was a poor abandoned creature. For the first time for years I was no longer alone, I was in communion. That had been my trouble. In living just anyhow, I had lost contact with other people, with God. Now I was in contact again, should I be able to set to work and build a real life?

I changed nothing, outwardly, in my life as a dancer and actress. But from now on all was subordinated to an inner reality, filled secretly with the love of God; and though, apparently, nothing was changed, my existence became bearable again. I remained on very good terms with the Mother Superior of the Dominican Tertiaries: she even came with her family to watch me dance, and thoroughly enjoyed her evening.

I had tried hard to go to Mass, to show my attachment to God, but I felt so out of place there that I decided to give it up. To do it for the sake of appearances was repellent to me, as I was sincere. After all, I needed no illuminated church in order to love God. My heart was as beautiful as a church. Of course I should have preferred to be a devout Christian, and accept all the rites, but I could not cheat and simulate what I did not feel.

A year went past like this. I had trouble with my health, but I was a very brave invalid; and all was well with me spiritually. Father H. came back to preach at the retreat, and I heard him with the same fervour. I ventured to speak to him when he had finished his sermon. I was worried by my lack of enthusiasm for Mass.

'Father,' I said to him, 'I feel I love God, but I feel I can't reach Him, I can't make myself go to Mass, it bores me to death, it seems too easy . . .'

Perhaps Father H. was touched by my sincerity. Usually, after his sermons, people came to congratulate him, as if he was an actor who had given a good performance. The women jostled each other round him, ogling him as if they were autograph-hunters.

'Not hard enough?' asked Father H.

'I mean that God deserves more than an hour at church on Sundays. I want to do more for Him . . .'

'What you must do is to kneel before Him lovingly. That is all. Lovingly.'

So that was all. To kneel lovingly at the feet of God. To let yourself go. Be docile. But I wasn't docile. I knew it. I was very conscious of it. I always had to force myself to do anything that seemed to require obedience. So now I fought to suppress this leaven of rebellion. That was why, one day, I went into St. Martin's Church.

It was dark and cool in there, and a feeling of total peace flooded over me at once. I was alone, walking slowly in the silence. I felt whole.

'It's simple,' I thought. 'I detest Sunday Mass because of the crowd of people, and all the trappings. But when I'm alone, in a church, I really feel that I'm in the House of God. It's all the other people that prevent my sensing His presence.'

I had discovered a bitter truth: I detested those other people, who deprived me of God. I refused to share Him. I was a monster of pretension and pride. I wanted to acknowledge it. I walked towards a confessional.

'Father,' I said, as soon as the priest drew the shutter aside, 'I am guilty of rebelling, and hating my neighbour. I should like to be shut up somewhere so that I didn't harm others. I should like silence and solitude for ever. Other people prevent me from finding God.'

He came out of the confessional, consternation on his face. He was an old priest, white-haired, tall and lean. He looked rather like a candle and his gaze was a warm and gentle flame.

'Come with me,' he said, 'and we'll have a little talk.'

He took me home to a very humble lodging. His maid brought us caramels. She was even older than he was, she seemed ageless.

I told him about my life, my troubles, my efforts to give fullness to my existence. He listened to me with immense benevolence.

'My poor child, there are two sorts of lunatics in this world, the priests and the actors.'

Like the Mother Superior of the Dominican Tertiaries, he, too, came to watch me dance. In the crowded Théâtre des Champs-Elysées he looked a little lost, but his eyes still kept the warmth of a living flame.

Early in 1952 I embarked on a difficult enterprise. With five friends, two men and three women, I decided to stage a ballet show. We had no money. We had to stir up the whole of Paris to find a theatre and scenery. We turned ourselves into painters, carpenters, publicists. I lost pounds in weight, and began to look like a skeleton. I was sustained by the thought that such physical expense might not be material wealth, but it should still please God by the unselfishness which it proved.

The show – I hardly need say – was a catastrophe. The first performance was postponed for a week because we were deserted by the boy who was to play the leading part; the show pleased a few amateurs who were mostly impressed by our faith and perseverance, but it left the public cold. Nobody came. Six months' efforts dissolved into nothing.

I left the friends I was living with, in Rue Pigalle, and went to the Porte Saint-Cloud, to a room that was lent me by a friend: I called her Fée and she was very fond of me. For some days I did nothing but eat, go for walks in the Bois de Boulogne and sleep. The first few nights I had to struggle against incessant nightmares. I used to wake up with a start, weeping bitterly, my throat constricted.

My brother was preparing to go to America, and he came to see me. He had been struck by the story of my failure. He advised me to join a company, to free myself from all the worries of production and administration.

'Just dance, that's all. Go on tour. Travel.'

'I think that dancing is really finished for me,' I said. 'I'm going to give the profession up, I want to leave Paris. I want another life.'

He must have thought that I wasn't serious, that I was only feeling disheartened and beaten. But as I spoke, I had suddenly felt I was really going to do it. I could no longer divide myself, have God in a corner of my soul and give my time to a profession which didn't satisfy me any more. God Himself did not lie. I would take a holiday, soothe my mind completely, wipe out the traces of a ruined past, and prepare myself. Prepare myself to live, from now onwards, only for Him.

. . . . .

I had to take practical decisions. Consecrating one's life to God was not so easy to do as to decide on. I had to choose an Order that conformed to my aspirations, get myself accepted. I didn't know how to begin. I wasn't going to set off at random down the streets, tugging at bell-ropes and saying: 'I want to put myself at the service of God.' However near they may be to heaven, convents must have their customs, like worldly institutions. They would hardly like strangers who arrived with fanatical ways. They certainly distrusted women who looked too much as if they had fallen from heaven. The easiest thing was to get information from the Mother Superior of the Dominican Tertiaries.

She thought I looked so happy I must be married. I explained to her that, on the contrary, I was ready to renounce that kind of ambition. I only wanted to love God; this decision was no sacrifice and seemed to lead to the greatest happiness one could dream of.

'I am not doubting your sincerity,' said the Mother Superior. 'I'm sure you are someone who can only live sincerely, but your health is uncertain. The Rules of all Orders are hard and physically wearing. Have you thought of that?'

I hadn't thought of that. I didn't think that sheer physical vigour could have any importance in an affair which concerned one's innermost soul.

'My body will have to obey,' I said. 'Dancing and acting also ask for robust health. I've succeeded in making my body do what I wanted so far, so I don't see why I shouldn't bring it to the service of God.'

'Are you specially attracted by any Order?'

'The Trappistines, or the Carmelites. And I'd prefer the Trappistines because they don't have recreation. I've heard of a Carmelite convent near Biarritz, where the sisters do nothing but cultivate roses in silence. I'm very anxious for silence. I don't want to shut myself up in a convent to hear the inanities of the other sisters and do needlework. Otherwise I might as well go on dancing. But Biarritz is at the end of the earth, and I haven't even got enough to buy a railway ticket.'

'I admire your ardour,' said the Mother Superior, 'but you mustn't act on the spur of the moment. Go to Nancy and see Father H. He'll advise you better than I can. He'll know what to recommend. How much is a ticket to Nancy?'

'It isn't so far,' I said. 'I could hitch-hike there.'

'Just as you please. But you can't set off like that. I'm going to give you a cheque. When you get to Nancy, try to get a room at the students' hostel.'

She handed me a cheque for five thousand francs and kissed me as if I was her daughter.

That was on 2 July 1952. That evening I wrote to Father H. to ask for an interview. He answered by return. He expected me any day after 2 August. I had a month to kill.

My friend, Fée, had rented a little villa on the Channel coast, at Cayeux. I decided to go there with her. I took some white linen slacks, a linen skirt, a yellow singlet, a bathing dress, the *Confessions* of St. Augustine and a copy of Father H.'s sermons. I was delighted to leave Paris. A sickening heat had fallen over the city, and the place had been given over to foreign tourists. All the windows were shut, the asphalt was melting in the streets, even the trees were withering. In the mist which hung heavily over the Eiffel Tower, the flag looked like a black banner, a signal of the plague.

2

The Last Holidays

THEY were strange holidays.

The house they had let to Fée under the pretentious title of 'villa' was nothing more than a shanty. We got out of the train, and walked through a square where a feeble fountain played, and then along a road which led over the fields to the sea. And there was the 'villa': we even mistook it for a hangar. I knew that I was preparing to leave the vanities of the world, comfort and luxury. I knew I was going to take a vow of poverty. But I could not restrain a feeling of disgust at the sight of this monstrosity of brick, mud, planks and sheet-iron, which greeted us, moreover, with a suffocating smell through the open door.

We stood dumbfounded for a moment; then, because the sun shone in splendour, because the waves were beating ten yards away, because the sunburnt bathers were laughing and playing with balls and hoops, we burst out laughing, too. Five minutes later, we had thrown our baggage pell-mell on the rickety table, and we ourselves were running towards the waves.

Next day, when the dirt had surrendered to a thorough cleaning with disinfectant, we found our house habitable. You only had to admit one convention: the picturesque. On the ground floor there were a big room and a kitchen. On the first floor, an attic bedroom, with a wooden balcony.

The décor – a grey-green sea, the dunes, sand, pines and sky. All in a heat that was worthy of the tropics.

I was there to wash away all that might still remain of a past that was useless to me from now on. I was there to be born again, to start once more from nothing. Every morning, in a bathing dress and a broad-brimmed straw hat, I wandered off into the pinewoods, and lay down. I didn't think about anything. I was part of a total symphony composed by God, just like the trees, the sand, the light and tides. The sun scorched my skin. I went back to find the meal that Fée had cooked. Fée certainly deserved her nickname.

She couldn't stay long at Cayeux. I was very fond of her, but I didn't feel sad to think that she was going. I was longing to be alone, or rather to be undisturbed, because I was no longer lonely, because I had God. It seemed to me I was impatient just like those couples who long for the guests to go so that the two of them can be happy together alone.

The arrival of Bill, an American friend of Fée's, unsettled me again. He meant to stay some time; and, when she left, Fée asked me to feed him. I was no cook, but I couldn't refuse my friend. And then Bill was a nice boy, a little bit mad, inoffensive, someone who could be somewhere without being noticed, a sort of invisible man. I made him some uninspired concoctions with rice, noodles and flour, and he ate them as if they were choice dishes. After a week, he left. This time I was free.

I arranged my life in an orderly way. I got up at six, and went to Mass. In the clear light of morning, I walked along the empty streets, crossed the deserted squares. There were only an old curé and a sleepy altar-boy in the church. I was in the seventh heaven. I no longer felt as if I were on earth.

I came back to the shanty dazzled; the air was still cool, and I breathed it in: it was a way of drinking in the skies.

To avoid the crowds – especially mothers and their children, swarms of children who were twenty times as irritating as dogs – I went to the beach in the lunch-hour. I went for walks along the shore in a bikini and a straw hat. I shut my eyes and let myself be guided by the fringe of the waves. I told my beads. I said to myself: 'Before the month is out, I shall be beside Him at last.' I picked daisies, and stripped their petals one by one to know how God loved me, how I loved Him, and it was always passionately, madly. The people of Cayeux, I learnt later, called me 'Miss Pin-up'. They saw me sunburnt in a bikini, and no doubt they took my solitary ways for scornful reserve. How could they have guessed that as I walked I was praying?

Sometimes, in the midst of this serenity, I was seized by such bursts of passionate ardour that I could no longer control them. In the fields, or among the dunes, I would cry out:

'God, I love You, keep me, don't leave me again! . . .'

Every evening I read a chapter of the *Confessions*. I rather envied Augustine for being able to talk of God so tenderly, and with such respect and intelligence, too.

'Forgive me, Lord,' I used to say as I shut the book. 'Forgive me: I have only my heart.'

I lived on rolls, chocolate and raw tomatoes. I slept a great deal. I had never felt so well.

I had noticed a chapel at the end of the beach. Late one afternoon when I had, as usual, done a great deal of walking, I went into it. It was cool inside. I knelt down on a wooden bench. It was time for Benediction. The harmonium sounded thin. There were old country women there, scouts, a few holidaymakers and two nuns. I looked at them attentively.

I thought: 'I am going to be like them, God, one of Thy servants . . .'

They were dressed in black, it looked ugly.

'Why,' I asked myself, 'why must they give such sombre clothes to those who walk in the way of the triumphant love of God? Why do they wear mourning when it is a marriage?'

I should have liked party dresses, lace, pearls, and brocade for those who were espoused to God! And not those robes of mortification which seemed to proclaim to the world that to consecrate one's life to God was to give oneself to a life of penance.

'And yet I am ready to be dressed like that, if need be. I am ready to obey. I am ready to nurse the sick, to tend children, to wash clothes, and sew, everything that I hate doing. I know that love must be paid for . . .'

I hardly knew anything about convent life, only the more or less fictional accounts that I had heard. I think that people rather like any impressions that reach them from these closed worlds, and they're ready to peddle about what they think they know. I was particularly alarmed, myself, by what I'd been told about cleanliness. It seemed that you washed as little and as rarely as possible, to show a disdain for all matters to do with the body.

'God,' I prayed in this chapel, where the chants hummed about me, 'God, I don't understand why I must be dirty to be near You. I am very willing to cut off my hair, to dress in black, to hide myself under a ridiculous head-dress, but I don't want to be dirty. You ought to understand. You Who washed the feet of the poor.'

July was nearly over. I thought about going back: I was

going to try to hitch-hike. The roads were crowded with holidaymakers' cars. At this time of year they readily stopped: the drivers were on holiday, free of care, and their good humour encouraged them to help their neighbours.

I put the house in order, wrote some letters, attended Mass for the last time and took leave of the old priest whose only congregation I had been for a month. He must have been curious about me. As I came out of the church, I found a driver who took me half-way to Paris and, without a moment's pause, told me every detail of his life as a young married man. Then, at the crossroads where he left me, I found a sporting type called Edward, who drove an ancient Chrysler with a folding hood, six yards long, at breakneck speed, and dropped me at the Porte de Saint-Cloud after asking me to lunch on the banks of the Seine. He made mild love to me, though he artlessly confessed that he was devoted to a lovely brunette and had lived with her happily for the last ten years.

3

Waiting

ON the 2nd of August 1952, at about one o'clock in the afternoon, in a trim white suit, and carrying a briefcase which held a few underclothes, toilet articles and some papers, I found myself once more on the station platform at Nancy, drowned in a khaki flood of soldiers, in the midst of a din of escaping steam, screeching brakes and shouted instructions, and tormented by such migraine that I could have screamed. My stomach was upset, my legs were dead. I was a wreck. I let myself be borne along by the crowd to the exit and asked for the Dominican convent. I took note, exhausted, of the 'turn to the right . . . take the avenue . . . a big round square . . . the tramlines . . .' and I set out, barely conscious. It was as hot as Hell.

I walked for a long time. I was dying of thirst, but I was walking in streets where there were no shops or cafés. I was no longer certain of being on the right road. The sun was pitiless. I almost shut my eyes so as not to see the glittering white walls of the houses. I wanted to collapse. I was at the end of my strength.

And yet, that morning, I had felt the exaltation you feel on days of momentous beginnings, the exaltation which makes you feel you can achieve the most extraordinary things. I had woken up early, leapt out of bed, drawn a deep breath at the window and there gazed on Paris revealed by a dawn like that of the first day of the world.

'It's the day of my true birth,' I had thought, then. And it had seemed as if wings were unfolding inside me.

The evening before, I had given away my dresses, books and trinkets, telephoned good-bye to those of my friends who were not yet on holiday, written letters to the rest. Behind me I left nothing but emptiness. I had burned all my boats with unashamed delight. I had fallen asleep the moment I had gone to bed. I had slept soundly. And now I was staggering through this endless city. Five hours in a train had been enough to put me in this state.

'Are you sure that your health? . . .' the Mother Superior of the Dominican Tertiaries had asked me . . .

My health. At the place I was going to, I should have to get up before dawn, work hard, sleep in winter in icy rooms, eat hardly anything. How could I stand up to this régime when a five-hour journey was enough to make me a wreck?

'It isn't possible,' I thought, 'that those who lack robust health should be deprived of the joy of serving God. It would be too unjust. Too cruel. It's only because the path that leads to Him is hard. I don't reject the hardship. I am ready to suffer to reach Him. I agree that tribulation should be demanded of those who want to approach Him. But I don't want it to be impossible.'

I had reached a building with closed shutters, surrounded by a garden. It was the address I'd been given. I rang the bell.

A priest appeared at a first-floor window, and leant out. I told him that I had come to see Father H. He replied that this was a hostel for young people, that I would find the Dominican convent at the other end of the city, at number 5 Rue de l'Oratoire. He raised his hand and withdrew his head.

This was indeed a calvary. Again I had to pass the houses, crushed by heat, I had to feel a more and more unbearable weight on my shoulders, feel the final spring give way inside me.

As I retraced my steps, I felt that this was a trial imposed upon me to measure my love for God. After all, it was better that God should not accept everybody. It was only right you should suffer in order to love and be loved. Since I was not very strong, and since I had to struggle to overcome heat and exhaustion, it was natural that God should choose to test me at my weakest point. As I recalled the thoughts of that morning, the thoughts that had made me see this journey as an easy, triumphal march, I shrugged my shoulders. I preferred a thousand times over that my love should be judged so fine that it could be tested by suffering.

As my spirits rose again, I decided to make certain of a lodging for the night, and to go first to the students' hostel. Luckily it was on the way to the Dominican convent, and I reached it half an hour later. It was a big building in a garden, at the corner of an oblong square, in which there were trees and street-lamps.

When I rang the bell a concierge came and told me the institution was shut for August. There was no one there but the bursar, Mlle Clotilde, I could try to see her, she was charming and might let me in as a favour. Mlle Clotilde had a black dress with a high neck, a tucker, chignon, and steel-rimmed spectacles; and she proved to be charming, put me down on her register, led me herself along the corridor and up the stairs to my room. It was small but bright, with a nice smell of fresh polish. She explained to me, clearly, where to find the convent I was looking for, near the cathedral. I thanked her, washed my hands, did my face, and set out once more. I was still tired, I still had migraine, but I was no longer miserable.

It must have been four o'clock. The heat was not so overpowering now. I had lost my appetite on the train, from watching some soldiers who ate cheese and sausage and drank bad wine all the way from Paris to Nancy. But now I began to be hungry, and remembered I'd eaten nothing that day. I bought a roll and a bar of chocolate, and as I swallowed the last mouthful, I found myself at the door of the convent.

The brother who served as porter let me in, took my name, and came back to say that Father H. would see me in three-quarters of an hour. I was too impatient to wait quietly in the cool chapel. I preferred to walk round the cathedral, where the bells seemed to be ringing merrily.

When I went back to the parlour, I knew Father H. was about to come in, and I imagined the scene that would take place, the scene I had come for. Father H. would ask if I'd changed my mind, I would say no, he'd open a notebook, give me an address, write a recommendation and bless me. Just then a door opened behind me. I turned round. I hardly recognized Father H.

The man I had seen with drawn features and sunken eyes, looking like someone who hadn't slept or eaten for days, was now a full-faced sunburnt man, as robust as a ski instructor. He noticed my astonishment:

'Yes,' he said, 'I took a month's rest and now I look like a human being again. But what about you, my child?'

I told him that I had put *finis* to my past life, that everything was arranged for my entry into a convent. I felt a burst of enthusiasm for him:

'Father, I don't trust the others, but I trust you completely.'

'Have you ever visited a convent?' he asked.

'Never.'

'Have you any idea of the Order you feel yourself specially drawn to?'

'I want an Order that imposes a vow of silence. The Carmelites would have tempted me, but I couldn't take the recreations. Is there a Trappistine convent in the district?'

'Not that I know of. I know one near Bordeaux. I could speak to the bishop about you. When do you think of entering?'

'As soon as possible.'

'I can phone the Mother Superior of the Poor Clares. Their convent is very near here. If she agrees, I believe that a little stay with her would be a good initiation. What do you think about it?'

I thought it was more than I had hoped for. Father H. phoned the Mother Superior of the Poor Clares, and arranged for her to see me next day. He asked me to let him know the result, and he blessed me.

'Go,' he said. 'Tomorrow I shall say Mass for your intention.'

I went back, overjoyed, to the students' hostel and dined alone with Mlle Clotilde. I told her about my life, and confessed that I was there to enter a convent. She told me there was a Trappistine house near Nancy, and the Trappistines there made a celebrated cheese; the students' hostel bought their cheese from them. After the meal, she suggested that I should take a stroll in the park.

It was growing dark. I wandered slowly among the clumps of trees, among the fountains. There was no one about, and silence reigned. I was the Sleeping Beauty in her own kingdom and I looked vaguely at the sky which had turned green. My migraine had disappeared, my fatigue had vanished. I felt happy. I remained happy until three N.C.O.s took it into their heads I was looking for adventures. They followed me in spite of my exhausted appearance and only left me in peace when I asked a lame passer-by to escort me back to the hostel. He seemed an extremely serious man. He had good manners, and said he felt ashamed to live in a town where men in uniform chose to behave so scandalously. I was on the point of defending them, of suggesting they might well deduce that a tanned young woman in a white suit, strolling casually in a public park at nightfall, might respond to smiles . . . But he was so convinced he had saved me from three villains that I should have spoiled his pleasure by making excuses for them. As he left me at the door of the hostel he ventured to ask me to tea next day, and arranged to meet me in a well-known cake-shop. I didn't dare refuse.

I fell asleep thinking of the day. I spent a very good night in my clean room with its nice smell of polish.

Next day I went to Mass at the Dominicans' in the Rue de l'Oratoire. Mlle Clotilde had a weakness for splendour, and she advised me to go to the cathedral. I chose simplicity. There was no frontal piece on the altar, only a large crucifix, with candelabra on either side; the priest officiated facing the congregation. For the first time in my life, I heard Mass offered in a way which had the sober beauty of a tragedy. I came out of the chapel convinced that the Dominicans were surely the *élite* of all men of God.

That afternoon, at the very moment the kind man with the limp must have been tying his best tie, I pushed open the door of the Poor Clares' convent, where the Mother

Superior was expecting me. Vespers was beginning. I went into the chapel, a tiny place as befitted so small a convent. It was impeccably clean, with whitewashed walls, simple woodwork and spotless windows.

I almost blocked my ears: behind a grille near the altar, the sisters were singing, and two hundred flayed cats would not have made a more dreadful noise. 'How dare they,' I thought furiously, 'how dare they believe that God has no ear for music?' I refused to give the smallest offering when an extern sister came and shook a purse under my nose at the collection; and I refused all the more firmly as she seemed a dreadfully pert minx to me, and during the whole of Vespers had knelt on the front bench, feigning holiness like a skilled actress. I agree that this wasn't a very good frame of mind in which to meet the Mother Superior of the convent.

They made me wait in a parlour not much bigger than a rabbit-hutch. After a few minutes, a panel slid aside and two faces appeared behind a grille. Both wore spectacles. One was old and peevish, the other pink and more prepossessing. I addressed myself to the old one, as seemed proper.

'I'm the young woman Father H. sent . . .'

'Yes,' said the Mother Superior, in a rat-like voice. 'Do you come from Nancy?'

'I come from Paris,' I said.

'Who are your parents?'

'My parents are dead.'

'What do you do?'

'I'm an actress.'

'And you want to enter a convent, just like that?'

She was almost having a fit.

'Yes,' I replied, quite unperturbed, telling myself I should manage it, 'I want to enter a convent.'

'It's quite impossible,' she proffered, 'you must change your life first.'

'I've come here to change my life.'

'But this is a convent; you don't go straight from the greenroom to the cloister. We only take young women we really know. We couldn't take you unless you spent a year here, at Nancy, and devoted yourself to some work . . . looking after abnormal children, for instance.'

I remained speechless. The spirit of revolt had slipped into me, slyly, under the pretext that the Poor Clares sang badly and that the extern sister had unbearable airs and graces. Now it had disappeared. Only this stark truth remained: they refused to allow me to enter the convent.

The Mother Superior guessed my confusion and grew a little more human.

'Since it's Father H. who sent you, we shall always be pleased to see you again. Come back and visit us when you want to.'

The peevish face disappeared and the pink cheeks and the youthful smile remained.

'Mother is right,' said the smile behind the grille. 'She wants to spare you the shock you would suffer if you were to change your life too abruptly. We are a very poor Order, you know. We have no servants. We iron, and sweep, and look after the garden ourselves. It would be too hard for you.'

She must have taken me for a middle-class girl who was having a fit of eccentricity and had to be treated gently. I wasn't going to explain to her. I went back angrily to the Rue de l'Oratoire, and told Father H. about my visit.

'They spoke to me mostly about housework,' I said, 'but not about God, they didn't mention Him.'

'I'm going to think things over,' said Father H., 'and pray.

Come back and see me in a few days, we'll try something
else.'

In a few days. He didn't understand that I had barely two
thousand francs left. But I couldn't worry him any more
and talk finance to him. He himself was living in another
world.

When I got back to the hostel, I knocked at the door of
Mlle Clotilde's office.

'I went to the Poor Clares, but they only take young
girls from Nancy. You mentioned a Trappistine convent
where they make cheese. Do you know where it is?'

'At U——. It's a village a few miles from Charmes.
There's a bus that will take you there.'

'I want to go and see them.'

'That's a good idea.'

Mlle Clotilde was delighted to see I had such a will to
fight. She must have decided that a faith which didn't
succumb to the first trial was worthy of notice.

Next day I set out on foot from Nancy, and decided to
hitch-hike. I still wore my white suit, and my hair was long
and wavy. It wasn't very honest to count on the effect that
this might produce on men to get myself free transport!
But I could hardly choose my means. Only two or three
cars came along: they didn't stop, and the motor-cyclist
who came to my rescue, when I'd already walked for hours
in the sun, certainly obeyed the dictates of pity and not
desire in taking me on his machine. Exhausted, perspiring,
wild-eyed, I could no longer inspire any other emotion.
Clutching this kind man's shoulders, and a little revived by
the wind in my face, I kept turning over some rather
incoherent ideas in my mind. I was a sort of Ophelia, someone was crying out: 'Get thee to a nunnery, go: farewell.' I
was running about the world, knocking at closed doors,

begging God to help me to find the one that was ready to open. 'Just one sign,' I said to myself. 'When I find the place where they offer me a glass of water I shall know they accept me at last, and even if the place does not please me, I shall stay there. Just a glass of water: that will be the sign I'm waiting for.'

4

Arrival at the Trappistine Convent

THE obliging motor-cyclist put me down at the bus-stop.
The bus took me to Charmes. And from Charmes I took
the road to U——. No one had been able to tell me exactly
if the village was two or twenty miles away. They knew it
existed, and which direction it lay in, and that was already
a good deal. I asked too much of them.

It seemed to me that since I left Paris I had done nothing
but walk, walk, walk . . . It was no good going on telling
myself that this endless walk was a marvellous symbol of
the quest for God, because my legs and feet did not agree.

After Charmes I had to trust to chance more than once
because there were no signs or milestones to direct me. I
went on between banks of tall grasses, between little woods,
and orchards, and the country was so hilly that I could
never see a whole sweep of landscape at once. Every time I
climbed a hill, I counted on seeing a village come into view,
but it was always another identical hill which I saw. I was
ready to give in to discouragement, to sit down and wait
for the improbable miracle, a car, a sign, whatever it might
be, the hand of God.

Then a cyclist appeared, came nearer, went downhill,
disappeared behind a curtain of trees at the bottom of the
valley I'd emerged from, and finally came round a bend
twenty yards from me. It was a priest. When he reached
me, he got off his bike: the hill was too steep for him. He

wiped his forehead and went through the usual dumbshow of a man overcome by heat.

'Monsieur l'abbé,' I asked him, 'is the Trappistine convent at U—— near here?'

It *was* near, very near. That little bridge on the right. A stony road. A gateway with a cross. I couldn't mistake it.

Heavensent abbé! If it hadn't been for him I should have taken the little bridge for a quite unimportant detail in the landscape and I should never have thought of crossing it. I thanked him, went off, turned round a moment to see him pushing his bike. It was just as he'd said. When I'd climbed a hilly road, all pebbles, I saw a cross shining over a gateway. There it was.

I pulled the bell-chain. A little door opened next to the main one. A nun's face appeared, she nodded, and said:

'Who do you come from?'

'I come from God.'

I said it automatically, because it was certainly true and because the question had taken me by surprise, without a prepared answer. The sister thought my reply a good one, and laughed. She let me in. I followed her through a well-kept garden, and went into a parlour.

'I'd like to talk to Reverend Mother,' I said.

'Reverend Mother is at Office,' answered the sister. 'Can you wait a few moments? I hope you haven't walked here?'

'Yes, I've walked from Charmes. I very nearly got lost.'

'Mon Dieu, and in this heat! Anyway, have you had lunch?'

Of course, as usual, I had eaten nothing.

'I'm not hungry,' I said, 'I'd rather have a glass of water.'

The sister vanished silently, and came back at once with a tray: on it was a glass of orangeade, and little cream cakes, bread and jam.

'I'll leave you,' she said, giving me the tray. 'Reverend Mother will come and see you as soon as Office is over. You have time to eat.'

I ate. I was really hungry. Then I put a comb through my hair and tried to think out the words I needed to convince Reverend Mother. It was important. My life could depend on them. But I was incapable of stringing three words together. A real dumb mute. My little remaining strength was used up in overwhelming emotion.

Just as had happened at the Poor Clares', a panel slid aside, and a face appeared behind a wooden grille. A round face, pink cheeks, big eyes, intensely blue, a short nose, and a smile. I was at ease at once.

I said, without any preliminaries, that I'd come from Paris because I wanted to serve God, that Father H. had sent me to the Poor Clares, that the Mother Superior had been shocked because I had been an actress, that I didn't understand why this had shocked her because, in my own soul, God had certainly passed straight from stage to convent. I spoke quickly, just as the words came to me.

'I'm in a great hurry. I want God at once and for ever. If you don't send me away, I think I shall stay . . .'

Reverend Mother listened benevolently. When I had finished, she asked me some questions. My family? A brother who was now in America. My origin? Russian ancestry; I had been born in Finland, but I was French all the same.

'For a year,' I said, 'every time I've asked a small mercy, I have been showered with mercies.'

'Yes,' she said, 'that is God.'

'This happiness is quite undeserved, but I can't do anything about it.'

She nodded.

'When did you last dance?'

'In June, but since January I've preferred acting. In the last months I acted just for God, and that sustained me.'

'Well,' said Reverend Mother, 'you really have come a long way.'

I added that I had no more possessions, I'd given everything away before I caught the train.

'Sister Marie-Joseph, the reception sister who welcomed you, will get you what you need. Stay here for a few days. Then we'll go on with this conversation.'

I thought of Mlle Clotilde. She would be worried about me. But I mustn't get bogged down in details like that. I said I was delighted to accept.

'One more word,' said Reverend Mother, gently closing the sliding panel, 'why have you chosen the Trappistines?'

'Because of the silence,' I said.

I was delighted by such a welcome, and I went back into the beautiful garden. There I found Sister Marie-Joseph again.

'So you've seen Reverend Mother?'

'She suggested I stayed here a day or two.'

'I've already got your room ready at the hostel. Anyway, you were in no state to go back this evening. You'll find some soap, a comb and a toothbrush. If you need anything, don't hesitate to ask me. Now I must rush off and get your supper ready.'

It was a wonderful convent. People did everything they could for you. Where was the famous Trappistine austerity? It was certainly not in this garden round me, this garden bursting with greenness and flowers, nor in the sweet-smelling wistaria along the top of the wall.

As I was looking for a bench to sit on, I saw the gardener coming. Here was the man who had planned this delightful corner. He was a fat, cheerful old fellow with stocky figure, wooden clogs, a straw hat, a blue apron, and a pug nose in the middle of a round, reddish face. He stopped beside me and nodded:

'Good afternoon, my child. If you need me, I'm at your service.'

I understood. He was not the gardener, but the chaplain. He confirmed it in the course of our conversation.

He was called Father Luke. He had come from the Trappist monastery at Tamiers, in Savoy, where he was Master of Novices. If he had this peasant-like appearance it was because the Trappist Fathers live by the work of their hands, as their Rule demands. He was none the less erudite for that. To hear him talk of his monastery, an old château with huge cold rooms and monumental staircases (he showed me photographs), I guessed that he regretted it and suffered from being deprived of its awe-inspiring austerity. He was pining away as a confessor of women. His calvary, so he told me, smiling, had lasted for six years!

'It's easier here. But for you it's better. The dormitories aren't so cold.'

I don't mind being cold, myself. In any case I shall never be able to compete with St. Thérèse.

When evening came, Sister Marie-Joseph, smiling as usual, brought me a copious supper.

I went to sleep very happy.

The Trappistine hostel, where I was installed, consisted of three parlours and a dining-room painted a curious pink. There were another parlour and five bedrooms upstairs, for visitors. I spent two days there in tranquil solitude.

The arrival of another postulant put an end to this euphoric monotony. A young girl from the north, Renée, from a very Catholic family of nine children, with a formidable reputation for respectability. I welcomed her with open arms. As soon as she came in you realized that she was stalwart, honest and straightforward.

Renée taught mathematics, and I wondered where, in that very round head of hers, she could really put algebra and geometry. Confronted with this star pupil, I persistently played the dunce. At meals I exchanged my soup and cheese for her dessert; and these deals, arranged in whispers in the big dining-room, sent us into great fits of laughter. I discovered later that a solid reputation for gaiety had preceded me into the enclosure.

Both of us led an existence ruled by the sound of bells. The thin little bell for rising. Bells at the beginning and end of Office. Bells at four o'clock, to announce the end of the day's work. The little repeated strokes of the Angelus. The little bell for rest.

We also learnt to follow Office in thick breviaries. You had to be very skilful to find your place: the Cistercian rite is complicated, you come and go, you always have to skip pages, turn back and start again. Renée knew straight away. As for me, while I was finding a Psalm, the voices that intoned it were off on another track.

We followed Office together. Renée never made a mistake. I often did. The feasts of the Church according to the Cistercian rite are intricate to follow. After every psalm you have to go and find the anthems on other pages, and finally come back to the main text and rush after the prayers scattered to the four corners of the psalter. It's a real gymnastic exercise for the fingers. I was skilful with my feet, but I was uncommonly clumsy with my hands, and only found the place at the word *Amen*.

Sometimes I completely mistook the Office and did not recognize a single word of the text.

When that happened, I went out filled with speechless rage, with tears in my eyes, ashamed of such stupidity. Father Luke and Renée consoled me, and assured me that they had known the same difficulties themselves.

We went to bed like chickens at seven o'clock. The morning is sweet in the country, not the slightest sound except the convent bell and the cock crowing in the distance.

At the end of every exercise there was a peal of bells, and so I began to be able to follow the way the Trappistines spent their time: the end of work at four o'clock sounded with a full peal, the little bell was for Vespers, three restrained strokes for the Angelus, and finally the little dormitory bells for rising and retiring.

I asked Sister Marie-Joseph:

'Can't we keep our watches?'

'No, the novices have no watches. As the whole day is regulated, you only have to follow.'

Sometimes I woke up with a start because a little bell was ringing in the middle of the night: the enclosed nuns were getting up already. I snuggled up under the bedclothes: how lucky, I could go on sleeping!

In the afternoon after None, which followed lunch in summer, Renée and I set out for a walk. One day we nearly got lost. We came back after nightfall. Father Luke and Sister Marie-Joseph, equipped with a lantern and staff, were just setting off in search of us.

'Reverend Mother came to see you,' said the extern sister, with her lovely smile.

'I'm very sorry, if I'd been told I shouldn't have gone out.'

'On the contrary,' she said. 'Enjoy your walks. Once you are enclosed, the walks are over.'

Next day, when we were about to set off, I asked Sister Marie-Joseph:

'Reverend Mother won't come back today, will she?'

'No, certainly not,' she answered.

U—— was a tiny little village with four or five houses, a post office, a *mairie* and a watering place kept exclusively for horses, the cows drank in the fields. I wasn't expecting so much green, the flowers struck a birthday note here, there and everywhere, and walking in the hot dust took on a charm of its own. We went on slowly, wilting even in the shade.

Renée knew nearly all the Trappistine convents in France. She had always been turned down. Once, however, she was nearly accepted but she hesitated and she didn't enter in the end. Now they didn't want her any more. Her best friend was a postulant in a Trappistine convent near Bordeaux. She was a former dancer from the Opéra who waited five years before she gave up dancing in order to be sure of her vocation.

I was worried by the coincidence.

A few days later, as we came back from a walk, Sister Marie-Joseph told me that Reverend Mother had sent for me, and would expect me next day in the parlour. 'We're going on with the talk,' I thought, and my heart suddenly beat faster. 'Perhaps I'm going to know what she thinks of me.'

I slept badly. I didn't usually hear the bell for the enclosed nuns, as it rang quietly at two in the morning. This time it woke me up. After that, I could only make brief plunges into a troubled sleep. I got up rather nervous and disturbed.

Reverend Mother appeared as she had done the first time behind the wooden lattice in the parlour. She didn't keep me waiting.

'You are accepted in the convent,' she said.

I saw, in her eyes, that she was pleased by the emotion she read in me. I stammered:

'But how did you know that I was worthy?'

'God Himself knows it,' she answered.

She gave me time to get used to the joy she was giving me. Then she asked:

'Can you tell me two people who can vouch for your good character?'

I mentioned Father H., the Dominican Prior at Nancy, and the Mother Superior of the Dominican Tertiaries in the Rue de la Glacière.

'She will certainly tell you my health is poor . . .'

Reverend Mother blushed; I had touched the crucial point.

'You know,' I admitted, 'I went eight years without setting foot in a church. I don't deserve such happiness.'

'You know what St. Thérèse said: "God is so good that He looks at faults between His fingers." '

I could have thrown my arms round her neck.

'I have been given so much these last months that a whole life devoted to His service won't be enough.'

'While you're waiting, you will lead the same life as our extern sisters: in the afternoon you will help them, the rest of the time you will go to Office, and for walks. You must get your health back; our life is hard, you must enter with reserves of strength. Don't forget that from now on you will be rising almost at the time you used to go to bed.'

'Not quite, all the same.'

'I would rather you went to the second Mass, the first is too early.'

'But I'm very well.'

She smiled.

'I ask you to go to the second Mass. From now on you

belong to our abbey, daughters must obey their mother.'

'When shall I be enclosed?'

'Not till your brother comes back. Have you written to him?'

'Yes, I've asked him to phone as soon as he gets my letter.'

'Let him come and spend a week here. Then you will enter. Next time I see you I'll introduce you to Mother Emmanuelle, the Mistress of Novices. I will see you soon. Good-bye, Sister.'

She closed the shutter again. She had called me 'Sister'. It was the first time. I ran out of the parlour. No, I should say I flew. I cannot remember now if I cried, or if I only thought I cried.

5

Postulant

'THIS is Mother Emmanuelle,' said Reverend Mother.

She left us. The Mistress of Novices was small, pink-cheeked, with spectacles and false teeth.

Mother Emmanuelle struck me, from the first words she spoke, by her extraordinary gentleness, I might even call it urbanity. She was a harmonious human being. I had never met one till then. I don't know which was the most remarkable: her calm, her balance, her entire renunciation of self, her perpetual self-control, or her harmony; probably it was all of them together. Her exterior fitted her inner self to perfection, not a crease, not a wrinkle.

She effaced herself to listen to me. From the first moment, I was her child. She accepted responsibility for my soul. She would have given her life for me. She would give it as generously for the next postulant that Reverend Mother presented to her. I pestered her with questions. I wanted to know everything about convent life:

'The secret of lasting happiness in religious life lies in blind obedience to the Rule and to your superiors. Consider yourself least, and obey in all sincerity when anyone gives you orders, even if it is the novice beside you. It is a perpetual act of faith; if they are wrong it is God's affair, yours is obedience. That is the secret of happiness.'

So spoke this woman after twenty years' enclosure.

Obedience. How simple it is!

44

'It is the only duty, it can even reach the point of heroism. The saints did nothing but obey, nor did Christ Himself.'

She spoke slowly, and it seemed to me she was writing straight on to my memory.

It is not difficult to approach God. You only have to let yourself be led. Mother Emmanuelle had a brother whom she dearly loved. The day she told him she wanted to be a Trappistine, he tried for seven hours on end to dissuade her. She was exhausted, but she didn't give in. He was furious that he couldn't convince her, and he never came to see her.

'Not even when you took the veil?' I asked.

'Not when I took the veil and not when I made my perpetual vows. I was sad about it. I am sad about it still.' My own brother, I thought, will never do that. He loves me too much. Of course, he'll regret it, too, perhaps he won't understand, but he won't say anything. I know him. And then, when he sees how I've blossomed, that will make everything all right.

'Have you been round the convent?' asked the Mistress of Novices.

'No, does it take long?'

'A good twenty minutes. We should have liked to enlarge it and buy the fields round about, but the peasants don't want to sell. When you go for your walk, climb the hill on the right, and take the path that follows the convent wall. If you go there directly after lunch, perhaps you'll catch sight of our Mothers. If I see you, I'll make a little sign.'

She didn't need to tell me twice. That day, I snatched my lunch, went out of the hostel, followed the wall and climbed up the hill. I turned round, the convent garden seemed very far away, perhaps I had climbed too high up. I came a little way down again.

Yes, then I could see inside.

I caught sight of a sort of small round chapel in the middle of the main path. The whole was built round a square. On the left there were trees, on the right there was a huge orchard, and at the far end of the fields there was a flowing spring. There was a green look about it. I cast my eyes over the whole estate. At last I managed to make out two minute dolls in white with tiny black veils, they seemed to be moving; it was a model on a very reduced scale. I couldn't have seen if someone had made me a sign. How stupid of me, there was a high wall! And they couldn't be looking. They couldn't see me even if they wanted to. I was too far away.

I felt a little as if I had tried to cheat, as if I had had a preview of what was kept for the elect alone.

I was moved. So there it was, the place that I should enter and inhabit. I didn't feel I was shutting myself up; on the contrary, I was going out of the world, beyond it, into space, I was free. I was going where my spirit led me; no, I was going in search of love. It was there that love was hidden.

I shut my eyes in ecstasy.

Look at it closely, this enchanting garden, this new Galilee. Neither Peter, nor John, was nearer to it, two thousand years ago. There it is: in a fortnight, . . . and even if I must go on waiting for six months, even if I must die at the gate, NOTHING will be able to separate us. I have everything. I only need to open my mouth: 'Behold the land flowing with milk and honey.'

How can it hurt me to obey? Even if they ask me to plant cabbages upside down. In any case I shan't know the difference. Since Thou art found in blind obedience, I shall blindly obey.

I went on with my walk. I went into the woods. I had to stay in the open air.

On the far side of the woods I found myself in more fields, right in the sun. I didn't feel the heat.

I came back to the convent, slowly, it was time for Vespers.

'Did you see our Mothers?' Sister Marie-Joseph asked me.

.   .   .   .   .

Renée had left a few days after they had announced my admission. When I told her that they had accepted me, she had shared my happiness. She felt a moment's sadness when she saw that once again the door remained closed to her, then she overcame her discouragement by thinking about her next attempt. I should have been incapable of such constancy, such submission. If I had been her, I'd have rolled on the ground, and screamed, and arraigned the world. Renée made no scenes, she admitted that the ways of the Lord are impenetrable, and that He might prefer someone with all the appearance of an evil spirit to one who was a model of virtue.

The very evening of her departure I had proved, moreover, that I was an evil spirit by dragging her off on a hare-brained adventure. Three days earlier, I had gone on an expedition with the extern sisters. Equipped with bread and butter, jam and chocolate, and armed with baskets, we had piled into the small van they used for delivering the cheese they made at the abbey. It was driven by a placid fellow with a large basket. Swift and silent as a commando patrol, we disembarked in a big orchard planted with mirabelle plum trees. The whole day, grimacing and puffing like a demon, our driver shook the trees with tireless fury while we went round on all fours, picking up, picking up, picking up, until we could see nothing round us, even when we shut our eyes, except a universe of mirabelle plums. We came back delighted and exhausted, our mission accomplished, with our loot of sugar and gold. Reverend Mother gave a cry of delight when she helped to unload our full baskets.

Next day I said to Renée that instead of picking flowers on our walks, we might equally well collect plums. And after gleaning at random, here and there, under the trees, we came back at twilight laden with an enormous basket. Father Luke grew pale when I told him about our exploit. It was pure and simple theft.

I told him that we'd already stolen the day before, with the complicity of the extern sisters; I told him we hadn't contented ourselves with fallen fruit, we'd shaken the trees, and Reverend Mother had even given the expedition her blessing.

'Yesterday,' said Father Luke, 'we had the owners' permission.'

'But,' I said, 'I thought that fallen plums were like mushrooms, they belonged to the first person who took them . . .'

Father Luke had to explain that everything on earth has its owner, that the peasants left the fruit like that to make it richer in sugar and prepare it for distilling.

'Remember this,' he said, 'that it is only in heaven that you can take things without committing a sin.'

It happened that the Trappistines were much loved in the village, and they could explain to the peasants that this was a Parisian's mistake. As for Reverend Mother, she had the tact not to say a word about it. Sister Marie-Joseph, who had a sense of humour, left a plate of the plums in my room.

I found it easier than I'd imagined to get through this extra month of waiting that was imposed on me before my actual entrance into the abbey. Mother Emmanuelle helped me a good deal. She told me what my life would be like in future. I would remain a postulant for six months.

The Trappistines are a contemplative and penitent Order who sing the praises of God seven times a day. This is their chief occupation, all the others are subordinate to it. *'Opus Dei nihil praeponetur,'* said St. Benedict. For fourteen centuries the monks have faithfully observed this rule.

The postulants' dress was black, ankle-length and they wore terrible little veils, edged with white. It was a severe test of one's vanity, but I did not care.

Six months later, you took the habit of novice or oblate. A white serge habit that reached the ground, wide flowing sleeves, a leather belt, like a soldier of God, completed by a heavy white serge cloak for Office. You also wore this for walks and studies, on Sundays, and whenever you weren't working. When you wore the cloak, you had to walk sedately: alone, or in line one behind the other, with your arms at your sides.

Every time you met a Mother or a Sister, you had to bow and smile.

'In the winter you may be cold, or in a hurry,' Mother Emmanuelle said to me, 'but you have to smile all the same. I call it a warming smile. It makes you come out of yourself. Good humour is very important. You will see,' she adding, smiling.

'I shall smile twice rather than once at someone I don't like,' I thought.

I came out dazzled by my conversations with Mother Emmanuelle.

I was learning my new vocation.

I had chosen the most austere, the most noble of Orders. The life had its own attraction. I became a member of a family of high lineage, attached to the court of the King of Kings. We were His maids of honour whose every gesture was laid down according to strict etiquette.

Our court dress was white serge, the harmonium our guitar, Latin our language. So I had to learn to walk and greet, to sing, and behave. It is not everyone who can enter a Trappistine convent, we are hand-picked. The novitiate would finally make me a member of this noble family.

The slightest movement became, in fact, a code of honour which one must live up to.

Everything assumed a divine – and dangerous – meaning.

There was not a second to lose, not a gesture to miss, not a thought to have except the thought of God. That was to be the rule of my life, that was why I had come.

To keep such a lofty promise, I could count on His help alone. He only would allow me to go to Him.

I was dizzy. My intuition was right: my life would be a long journey in search of Him. The nearer I reached Him by the purity of my life, the better I should see that He was far away. My longing to attain Him would grow continually as the years went by.

Of course I did not understand all this in a day, but with every visit from Mother Emmanuelle a point was clarified. Some human beings can talk to you about the weather, and their radiance, their mere presence will still enrich you.

.   .   .   .   .

My brother phoned me from Paris, he had just found my letter. I gave him Reverend Mother's invitation to come and spend a week with me at the convent. I felt that a week would seem too long to him, and, in fact, he only stayed three days.

We went for long walks, which I found very tiring, but I didn't dare tell him so. He had come for such a little while.

'You're sure you won't regret the dancing?'

'What a question!'

'Why shut yourself up when there are so many sick people to look after?'

'So you say that, too! But I'm not meant to be a nurse. I'd only have to touch an invalid and he'd die at once!'

I told him about my visit to the Poor Clares.

'But,' he said, 'it's more useful to serve hot soup than to shut yourself up.'

I thought that was so absurd that I didn't even answer. I just didn't see the connexion between God, Whom I was seeking, and whether or not one gave out hot or cold soup.

He added, calmly:

'Don't you think it's a little egoistic to shut yourself up all alone with God and let everyone else go?'

'Yes, if we led an easy and pleasant life here, but we don't. I shall be cold, and in Lent I shall be hungry; we work hard and give everything to the poor. That is another way of serving hot soup. In the eleventh century, travellers' feet were washed and the Abbé made them sit at his right hand out of his great charity. We don't beg, we earn our living like everyone else, and we pray for everyone. It's our right to live as we see fit, after that. You must accept contemplative vocations.'

He didn't say anything. He was unconvinced.

I added:

'I believe that in any case outside works are only one way of serving God. All paths lead to Him. I have found mine. I cannot and will not follow any other. I have read the Rule:

it is perfect. Tell me another organization that would "hold good" without fail for fifteen centuries? Does the Order of St. Benedict need nothing but showers, refrigerators and phones to be up to date? Life is so balanced here – prayer, manual work and anthems – that no change has been necessary.'

.　　　.　　　.　　　.　　　.

We came back slowly from one of our longest walks, the last.

We had stopped talking.

He was to leave next morning at dawn. He didn't want me to wake up. We must avoid emotion. We should never be able to kiss each other again, or to take each other's hand. I should never be able to look so closely into his face again, gaze at him as I was doing.

I tried to be gay. I didn't want him to think of all that.

After dinner I told him that I was happy here, that I loved God, that my love for my family would only be the stronger for it.

Reverend Mother assured him that they would take good care of me, and asked him to come and see me at Christmas.

I cleaned his shoes before he went to bed.

When I got up, he had gone.

.　　　.　　　.　　　.　　　.

To my astonishment I did not yet enter the enclosure. They didn't even mention it to me again.

Mother Emmanuelle gave me some drawings to transfer; she was making a breviary like the old monks used to make in the Middle Ages.

Reverend Mother had had a warm testimonial from the Dominican Mother Superior, but also a warning about my poor health. Luckily this letter had no influence on her, she was determined to take me come rain come storm.

She had decided, but in the meanwhile I was standing waiting at the door. It was a real trial. I confessed as much to Father Luke:

'Are you sure they still want me?'

'What an idea! Don't you know that Father H. is at Lourdes? He's written to say, "Whatever you do, don't let her go".'

A few days later, Reverend Mother said to me:

'You will be called Sister Bernadette.'

'Can't I keep my own name?'

'It's certainly pretty, but we have no saint of that name in our Order. I think that Bernadette suits you very well.'

She repeated to me several times:

'Our life is hard and full of trials, but we have chosen it.'

An unpleasant little shiver ran down my spine.

I thought:

'What's the use of repeating it to me, I shall certainly find out. I don't want any cold water thrown on my enthusiasm. I am seeking God, nothing will seem disheartening in my search for Him.'

They gave me work to do where it was warm.

'Anyway, I'm not going to spend the whole winter outside!'

I let life go on in its own way.

I took advantage of my freedom to write to my brother. He had had a terrible journey with five or six changes of train before he arrived in some part or other of the world where they were covering goodness knows what.

While I was waiting I went on attending Office. I helped

the sisters in the hostel or drew when we didn't go out. I read enormously. I was so anxious to learn. I didn't know where to begin. With St. Paul: Father Luke's special subject. He brought St. Paul to life for me, this bald little man with the broken voice who undertook extraordinary journeys so that he might bring good tidings to the world. I was fired by the thought of this stunted man with the beguiling tongue who converted so many people to Christ.

One evening, after Vespers, someone rang at the convent door. Two gendarmes were asking to see the young lady from Paris.

Sister Marie-Joseph was terrified:

'They want you in the storeroom.'

I found the country policemen there, wearing the sort of hats that children make out of newspapers: the same model but plain black. Polite and embarrassed:

'You've come from Paris?'

'Yes.'

'You're working at the convent?'

'No, I'm on holiday.'

'Because if you're working there, no one's registered you. But if you're on holiday, that's all right.'

'Yes, I ought to be entering the convent any minute.'

'Ah, the convent. Thank you, Mademoiselle, do excuse us.'

They went out and put on their hats again.

'I thought it was about the plums,' said Sister Marie-Joseph.

I laughed:

'It's much funnier than that, they thought the convent was employing me. Employing me how, I wonder?'

I had a letter from Renée. I told her about our potato expeditions.

'They didn't take her,' I said to Father Luke. 'Why is that?'

'She's not as free as you.'

September was drawing to an end, it was beginning to grow cold. On certain mornings, after Mass, I changed, slipped on some boots (I was not a little proud of them) and we went into the fields just behind the village.

The beetroots had been dug up and lay in rows as far as the eye could see, earthy, and lightly covered with a coat of frost. They had to be cleaned and heaped up in piles. Your hands grew numb, your fingers blue with cold; but this mortification vanished with the first ray of sunshine. Then the workers from the convent came to pick up the beet with the tractor. At ten o'clock we drank boiling hot coffee, the hardest work was over, we were warm at last.

The village people began to know me; they called me 'the postulant from Paris'.

One day, as I was coming back from a walk, I was caught in such a downpour that I had to take refuge under a tree. I waited some time, but it thundered and rained so hard that I thought it better to run back to the convent as fast as I could, rather than get drenched.

And to think I'd refused Sister Marie-Joseph's umbrella! It was so ugly!

Next day I was in bed, but Sister Marie-Joseph looked after me so well that after two days I got up again and went on with all my work. They didn't send me outside to scrub vegetables any more; I peeled them in the hostel. I was also given a little dusting to do. My clumsiness delighted Father Luke.

The convent trusted me. I took the letters to the post; it was one of the best-kept houses in the village. You put the packets down on the corner of the mantelpiece or on the table with the knitting. The postwoman knew I was going to be enclosed any day and she looked at me with a mixture of sympathy and commiseration. The enclosed nuns were loved in the neighbourhood, but people credited them with alarming penances: wearing hairshirts or whipping themselves with chains. The one word 'Trappistine' put people into a state of panic. Ignorance only increased the mystery.

One morning there was a knock at my door:

'There's a visitor for you.'

What a pity, I was just going for a walk.

It was Fée. Worn out by the journey, starving, upset and terrified as well. The combined emotions had so exhausted her that when we had got a room ready and warmed, we put her to bed. She slept there till the evening. Reverend Mother came several times to welcome her, but she was still asleep.

Next day was sunny. Out in the country, Fée explained that she wanted to take me back to Paris. She was certain of convincing me and bringing me back to reason. Great was her astonishment when I told her I had decided to stay at the convent. I tore up a telegram from Sacha Guitry, and an offer for a tour, without even reading them.

Poor Fée burst into tears, and reproached me for deserting my profession. She wanted to go home at once:

'You haven't got the purity of a Pitoeff, poverty terrifies you. I realize it's useless to argue.'

.   .   .   .   .

The meeting with Reverend Mother was an epic. Fée was sobbing. I felt as hard as an executioner. I assured Reverend Mother I hadn't beaten her!

Fée had also brought me a quantity of food: I staggered

under the packets of nuts, chocolates, fruit and cakes, completely nauseated. If there was someone who longed for Lent, it was certainly me.

The imperturbable Robert drove us to the station.

It was the beginning of the autumn. The brilliant colours had vanished. Everything had turned to rust, sober green, yellow, grey. The hills were covered with sombre shadows. I had not travelled the road in this direction before, and it seemed to me all the more beautiful.

I told Fée about my arrival on foot at the height of summer. She just had time to get her ticket, the train was coming in.

What a relief! I was finding it more and more difficult to talk to lay people. From now on the only people I would have anything in common with were religious.

The driver had errands to do for the convent, I had an hour to wander round the town. The lights in the shops were going on, one by one, people were looking into the windows; compared with U——, it seemed to me like New York.

Quick, let's go back to the convent! What was I doing here?

We went back in utter silence. Robert was well trained, and behaved as if he was alone.

And then the waiting began again. I was not the least impatient. I knew I was where I belonged. Since I was still a nun only in intention, I tried hard to please God. I felt serene, relaxed, full of hope and certain of the future. Rather like the young peasant girl who has pleased the prince.

I began slowly to appreciate my happiness.

I saw Mother Emmanuelle again one day:

'Do you think I shall enter soon?'

'Of course.'

She said no more. I knew she thought about me.

Father Luke came to me in great delight and announced:
'It's arranged for the fifteenth of October.'

'No, is it really true?'

'Reverend Mother told me.'

The evening before I was due to enter, he sent for me:

'Father H. has written. He has been kept at Lourdes by the sick, and he's not coming back to Nancy till the end of the month. He begs us to wait for him before we enclose you.'

'To Hell with Lourdes, and the sick, and Father H.! Why should I need him? I can easily do without his benediction. I came to the convent quite alone, I can certainly enter it the same way.'

Father Luke laughed to see me so angry.

'Poor man! He's very fond of you, you can't refuse him this.'

'Father, it wouldn't matter if they had fixed a date for me, even next July. What is terrible is this constant postponement.'

I added, jokingly:

'You are quite sure that Reverend Mother hasn't changed her mind?'

Every convent of enclosed nuns is under the absolute authority of Reverend Mother. In the convent she represents Christ and must be obeyed accordingly. She is herself under the authority of a Visiting Father, the abbé of the monastery on which the nuns depend.

We had a visit from him. He asked to speak to me. Because my health was delicate, they decided I should be an oblate.

I was grieved I could not make vows. I had a sense of cheating, of being only half accepted.

My eyes were still red when Reverend Mother summoned me to the parlour:

'I felt that Sister Bernadette was going to be sad. It's always the same story. We want to give God what we want ourselves, but He acts according to His own designs, and we find it hard to accept them.'

'I want all He wants. Tears are just sentimental.'

'And I was bringing you your habit.'

A long, shapeless, black woollen habit, sumptuous in my eyes.

'You are to try it on. They'll shorten it for you so that you don't billow too much. Here is the black veil that goes with it. We'll open the door of the convent to you at three o'clock on the eve of All Saints' Day.'

I was speechless.

'Father H. will come and see you on Friday, we've invited him to spend the afternoon at the convent.'

I wrote to my brother at once.

'Pray for me, I am being enclosed at three on Saturday.'

From Thursday onwards I had no sleep. I read the Gospels as if there would be no Gospels to read in the convent.

They shortened my robe. They cut off my hair. I noticed that it was a pretty colour.

My brother had sent me some black nylon stockings. It was icy. On Friday morning Father H. arrived with his Paris face: in other words a very weary expression. He told me he was pretty tired after his journey from Lourdes. He had kept vigil, preached, tended the sick. I still remembered how he had spoken of Our Lady in the first of his sermons that I had heard.

I imagined that since he'd been one of the first to know

of my quest for God, he was going to say some inspiring things to me. I was moved. He had come so far to see me!

Instead of that we chatted happily about one thing and another. I told him I'd had a letter from him addressed to me in Paris.

'Yes,' he said, 'I didn't know where to find you. When Reverend Mother wrote that you had been accepted and asked my opinion of you, I understood you had found what you sought. I had prayed a great deal.'

'It's funny, I didn't have the impression that you'd thought about me so deeply. I'm touched.'

'Well, now,' said Father Luke, coming in, 'have you finished your spiritual conversations?'

The two priests went out.

'One more night,' I thought, 'one more dinner. To-morrow, at three o'clock, I shall be *inside*.'

Three o'clock, the hour at which Christ had died, and the hour when my mother had died, too. She had died on a Friday at three o'clock. She had grown white and hard as stone.

What's going to happen tomorrow at three? I ate my lunch like a sleepwalker. I went up to my room.

Father H. came to say good-bye to me:

'Father, give me some advice. You took Orders at seventeen . . .'

'You don't really know what you're doing at that age,' he said to me, smiling. 'Let things take their course, let things take their happy course.' He made the sign of a little cross on my forehead and climbed into the convent van.

Had I really needed to wait a fortnight for him?

'He preaches so well,' I told Father Luke, 'and he didn't open his mouth here. Why?'

'No doubt you've no need of it,' said Father Luke,

joking. 'He'll come and preach here at the Easter retreat, you'll see him again.'

He added:

'I warned the sisters that you are very sensitive to cold, so that they'll give you more blankets on your bed. You mustn't feel the cold if you don't have to.'

I went up to my room to put my things in order. I only had my briefcase, my white suit and old striped slacks.

I asked if I could wash. Yes, there were showers; you could have one every day, but apparently you couldn't spend much time over it. Everything was regulated. So you stripped yourself of everything, even of time.

I had no fountain pen, or watch, or notepaper.

I kept my brother's photograph. There was no need to tear anything up.

Thou knowest I am not pious. I don't care about all that – I want Thee. And for Thee I am ready to sacrifice everything.

In fact, I give nothing and have everything. Thou, Lord, must be the loser with Thy creation.

6

The First Day

I HAD a strange dream. It was Sunday and they hadn't come to fetch me. I had missed a day, the only day, the one important day of my life. Could it be that I hadn't woken up? Why hadn't Sister Marie-Joseph come for me? Had I slept for two and a half nights without meaning to? It was too cruel. I struggled and floundered on the verge of despair. Slowly I returned to consciousness. Still in my dream, I said to myself: 'No, it's a nightmare, I feel it's a nightmare; yes, of course, it's Saturday today.' I continued to struggle so hard that I woke up.

The bells were ringing for second Mass; I just had time to put on my postulant's robe and rush into chapel.

I was so glad that I'd come out of my nightmare at last, that I laughed out loud as I went down the stairs. I passed Sister Marie-Joseph, who'd been worried not to see me. My laughter reassured her.

I got as near the grille as decency permitted. My mind was so strongly impregnated by the sense of separation that if they'd assured me that on the other side they didn't breathe like us, they didn't eat like us, that they were transformed into spectral nuns, I really think I should have believed them.

I cast a brief glance towards the grille. In a moment, now, I should be there, I should see. Would you feel the same curiosity when you were on the other side? There would be the moment of transition, the moment you changed your skin. You would become a new being, curious about the future, not the past.

I caught sight of some wooden stalls. I knew Reverend Mother's was on the left for the first Mass, at the back for the second. She was in her place and she was praying for me. I had a friend, too, at the end of the choir, on the left.

Sext (the sixth hour) followed Mass. I humbly recognized that I hadn't seen or heard or followed anything. Could it be that they were singing Sext already?

How do you expect me to hear what is happening on earth? Quick, Lord, a tent, just one, there's none but me! The chapel was deserted, the enclosed nuns had gone. My breakfast was cold.

'I was wondering if you were going to come. Make the most of this last bread and butter,' said Sister Marie-Joseph, smiling.

'Don't you ever have it on the other side?'

'Yes, at Easter, Christmas and Pentecost. On Reverend Mother's feast-day you'll even have a wonderful lunch.'

I looked at the parlour where I had enjoyed so many fits of laughter with Renée, so many meals. I looked at the garden. The wistaria had faded. I went into the room where they kept the big cupboard full of china for relations' reunions. One day, when he was cleaning, Father Luke had nearly knocked it over. There had been a terrible crash. We'd opened it with beating hearts: all the glasses were one on top of the other, the plates were leaning over dangerously, but nothing was broken.

In my room, the briefcase was ready, my few belongings tidied up. *Jésus en son Temps* by Daniel-Rops. I hadn't even started to cut the pages. I seized the book of the Gospels Father Luke had lent me. I was going to be enclosed. This was not the moment to go out. Enclosed, the word was magic. I saw flagged walks, a fountain, Gothic windows delicately carved, and silence over all. It would be very funny if the cloister was frightful, with toads and not a blade of grass.

The Angelus rang the three regulation peals . . . lunch . . . I should have liked to grasp the minutes in my hands. No, they were not mine. And yet, here, everything was mine and I had no right to touch it. It was two o'clock. At three o'clock, if she was punctual, Reverend Mother would come and fetch me.

At twenty-five past two, I heard the sound of footsteps. It was Sister Marie-Joseph, who said to me:

'Quick, they're there!'

I ran to the enclosure door, the one they only opened for postulants. I entered. Reverend Mother and the Mistress of Novices received me on their knees. I was overcome and horrified. Received by two dwarfs on their knees. It was monstrous.

Happily, they rose to their feet and led me to the chapel. I followed them. A staircase, a landing, a great deal of white: the novitiate. A little corridor, one might almost call it a recess, the Mistress of Novices' study. A clothes-horse of a woman was sweeping it. They made us kiss each other; I was not at all embarrassed, I wanted to. My little black veil was put on. Reverend Mother's eyes were laughing: she traced the sign of the cross on my forehead and vanished. They led the way to the dormitory. It was nearly a hundred yards long. The walls were wooden, and our mattresses were separated from each other by half partitions of wood and cut off from the central passage by white curtains.

The Mistress of Novices pointed out my 'bed'. Over the curtain there was a wooden bar, and on it was written 'Sister Bernadette'. When you had pronounced your vows or taken your veil, the name was engraved. Mine was only written.

We passed a professed nun. Mother Emmanuelle made strange signs to her, the nun brought a cord and they stretched it behind my bed, or rather my mattress, for hanging up hand-towels, and propping up the tooth-glass. My domain was less than four feet wide. In the wooden part of my bed was a drawer for a change of linen and the bare minimum of toilet articles. There were also a pail, a basin, and a chamber. On the wall there were two wooden mushrooms, on which to hang my cloak and Sunday robe.

It was icy cold. There was a nice smell of pinewood. I could imagine myself in a mountain châlet. Everything was meticulously clean. Mother Emmanuelle led me into her study. I glanced out at the vast gardens outside, stretching to the fields. The window was shut. The room was slightly heated. Unlike the dormitory it felt pleasant. Mother Emmanuelle gave me advice which I scarcely heard.

They showed me my place in the novitiate, a big room with whitewashed walls. There was a table in the middle, and on either side was a sort of long bench, with little lockers underneath it for our few personal belongings. There were also a bookcase and a little altar dedicated to Our Lady. Every novice had her own place on the bench. Two enormous bay windows looked over the convent garden; and, seen at noon, it was a very bright room. We were separated from the community (we only met them at meals and devotions, and sometimes at work), and we were nursed, and guided, and taught with zeal and love.

I was able to keep my letters, photos and books in my locker. It was strictly forbidden to open anyone else's locker, on pain of dismissal. And everywhere there was utter silence. Not a sound, literally, not one. Well, perhaps bird-song. I'm not sure about that. My heart was beating. I was in the House of God.

The bell rang for Vespers. The ritual had been explained to me, and my experience at the gate was useful. Otherwise I think I should have been lost.

Scarlet with confusion and timidity, I followed the file of nuns as they made their way towards the chapel, one by one. We novices, oblate and postulant, must always make way for them. I was the last. No, the last but one. Surrounded like that, there was less risk of my going astray. The solemnity of the enclosed nuns entering the chapel struck me with fear and admiration. I sang boldly at the top of my voice. I hurled myself into the psalms. I had a vague feeling that I should be scolded for it when we came out, but no matter, my heart was too full.

The harmonium was silent. It was time for meditation. I don't know what I was thinking about.

Reverend Mother tapped on her stall with her finger, a brisk little tap: the community went out, noiseless and erect. One after the other, the long file of enclosed nuns made their way towards the refectory. They went forward soundlessly, their heads held high, their arms stiffly at their sides. There was such dignity about it, that it seemed like a procession.

It was in the spirit of humility that we rose during the night. We had to work during the day and go to rest when the sun went down.

It was dark and I groped my way along. I was not looking, but I felt we were going along the cloister. Ghost-like, we entered an enormous room. It had a high ceiling, bare white walls, and a big crucifix over Reverend Mother's table. She sat alone, facing the long rustic tables, which were set out in four rows. Reverend Mother reached her place and gave the signal for the *Benedicite*. I followed the prayer on my paper.

I was sitting next to the Mother who would supervise my work. I felt the eyes of the whole refectory upon me; I was the new postulant. My throat was so constricted that I couldn't swallow a thing except the black coffee which the lay sisters served us. After coffee, on the days when we didn't fast – five times a week – Grace was said aloud and there was a reading. We had to ask Reverend Mother's permission to leave the refectory. Wednesdays and Fridays, when there was no reading, the *Benedicite* was said in a whisper and we could leave when we wanted to. So I was obliged to be patient. I didn't understand a word of what the novice was reading in her high-pitched voice. I hoped it wasn't Latin. It was French, but read in an unbroken monotone, without punctuation or feeling. I tried in vain to listen.

We went up to the novitiate again.

'Your emotion has spoilt your appetite,' said Mother Gertrude, laughing.

She was a beautiful girl with mocking green eyes, a turned-up nose and dimples. She had the figure of a mannequin.

I was presented to all the sisters of the novitiate: Mother Aleth, a young professed nun, Sister Isabelle, the clothes-horse of that afternoon, and Sister Marie-Raymond, whom I promptly nicknamed Sister 'Piglet': a heavy Alsatian peasant-woman, with gappy teeth and pink cheeks. I discovered later that she had a sense of the comic, was tough, and knew herself to be slow-witted, which she found most humiliating.

I had quite a struggle before I succeeded in thinking Sister Raymond, not 'Sister Piglet'.

Everyone kissed me, Mother Emmanuelle was there and Mother Gertrude, too. Reverend Mother rushed by like a whirlwind. As for us, we kissed each other in absolute silence, and the silence remained unbroken. No one in the novitiate knew that I came from Paris, or that I had been in the theatre. I was Sister Bernadette, postulant, and that was that.

A bell rang: it was time for the reading before the last Office. I put on my cloak, with great difficulty, my veil got in the way. The others did it easily: they were used to it.

Nearly all the community were already in the cloisters when the novices arrived. We bowed low to right and left and sat down.

The reader was opposite Reverend Mother's chair. I didn't envy her. I couldn't have articulated a sound. My throat was still constricted. I wondered how the air could get through. This time I understood what was read, and that was much better. The reading lasted twenty minutes, then we went and said the last Office of the day. It was sung in psalmody in the shadow, only the singer on each side of the choir had her lamp lit. They ended with the *Salve Regina*. The chapel was now quite dark: only the statue of Our Lady on the other side of the altar grille was illuminated. We remained on our knees a few minutes. I was bursting with joy and gratitude, and tried to quiet the beating of my heart.

Reverend Mother stood at the door of the chapel and a novice handed her a holy-water sprinkler. Every professed nun, novice and lay sister passed, bowed low and received the blessing of the mother of the family before she went to rest. Silence is the rule all day, but in the dormitory it is exacted to such a point that, if fire broke out, you would

have to say so in a whisper. St. Benedict, the founder of
our Order, threatened the severest penalties for the monk
who failed to observe this imperious command.

From the few hours I had spent within the cloister I could
already understand how admirably personal freedom was
respected. Life was communal but you were alone in your
search for God. And God was not to be found in tumult.
Once upon a time, He spoke to those who loved Him in the
desert, today He spoke in the silence of their hearts.

I drew the curtain of my cubicle.

The nuns slept fully dressed, but as a postulant I still had
a right to my nightdress. It was cold, and I curled myself
up in a ball. There were a rough white sheet and three
blankets on the mattress; and a tiny doll's pillow. I put
everything I possessed on the bed to get warm.

As an exception I was to go to Matins tomorrow. All
Saints' Day is one of the greatest festivals of the year.
Mother Emmanuelle had explained Office to me, but in the
choir there were enormous and unmanageable books of
psalms. Happily there would be two of us following the
text, for I completely depended on my neighbour. Without
her, I should have been lost.

In my mind, I went over the second half of yesterday.
There was a restrained though very real delight floating in
the air. But it was not Christmas yet. I was glad that I'd
been born. I went to sleep.

Someone scratched at the partition. It was pitch dark. I
leapt out of bed. I could hardly open my eyes, but my soul
was ready.

I was on the stairs at once. Shadows passed me, preceded
me, followed me. We entered the choir. In the high stalls
(some of them already lit) the enclosed nuns were getting
the books ready. The mother organist, who played the

harmonium, was in her place, turning the great psalter on its pivot.

Then Reverend Mother gave the signal, we bowed to the crucifix and the feast began. We sang everything: psalms, anthems, versicles. Only the lessons were read – there were twelve of them – by twelve nuns at the rood screen. Before each lesson Reverend Mother gave her blessing. We followed everything in our breviaries. After three lessons, the chants began again. Two nuns went to the middle of the choir to chant the responses. Like great albatrosses with white wings, they bowed towards the altar, went to the harmonium, bowed to one another, bowed to the altar again and began the response. We responded to certain passages.

Everything seemed to happen with extraordinary speed. It was no longer an earthly feast, our friends in heaven had come to lend their voices. It was no longer forty of us singing, it was legions. A single voice that swelled and filled the whole world. A single soul. Let each of us rejoice, it is the feast of all the saints, of all the elect, of those who are happy for ever. For them it is the feast eternal and we are joining in it with them. It passed like a hurricane of happiness.

We were not only moved, we were carried away, possessed, converted. We only wanted to stay there until the end of the world.

At last it was over. Lauds, a final hymn, a solemn prayer said by Reverend Mother. A signal, and we all bowed to the altar. We left the chapel and went upstairs to wash in the dormitory.

Day was dawning. It was pale grey, but, for me, it was silver. I was not sure that all this was real.

I warmed my feet in hot water. So I was still on earth.

Unfortunately, I hadn't got a lovely white cowl but an old grandmother's bonnet. But if it pleased God, that was all that mattered.

According to the custom of solemn feasts, we stood near the screen for the first Mass.

I could see Father Luke's back. I knew that he was saying Mass for my intention. But did I really need that? I already felt so secure. I was enclosed with God, but it would be a pity if something happened to me all the same.

After Mass they pushed the great wooden panel across the screen. So separated from the world, we began Prime, the first Office of the day; then we went to the chapter-house. The martyrology was read in Latin and *recto tono*. I'm blessed if I understood anything. Then a point of the Rule was read, and Reverend Mother made a brief comment on it. The whole community was gathered together: professed nuns, novices, the oblate, the postulant and the lay sisters, ninety in all. The lay sisters had brown cloaks.

Duties in the refectory and choir were given out and a reader appointed. These things were usually done by novices as soon as they were thought capable of doing them. I hoped I should never be.

We went into the refectory. There was butter and a big round slice of fresh bread at each place. I could not bring myself to eat. I hid the food under my napkin. Milk was passed round, the sign of a great feast.

I had a bit of paper with a copy of the prayer said after meals. It was Sunday. A fine day. Mother Gertrude took me off on a very short tour. The bell for High Mass was already ringing. It was impressively sung.

We stood in the stalls, with our backs to the wall, only turning towards the altar when the celebrant raised his voice. During the *Pater* the community bowed down, their

hands on their knees. Before Communion they seemed to
crumple: prostrate, their foreheads near the ground, the
body resting on the second knuckles of the fingers . . . On
all fours before the Lord. Why not? Well executed, this
ceremony was not lacking in grandeur.

Mass lasted nearly an hour, it didn't seem long to me,
nothing seemed long to me . . . When we went out there
was a great reunion at the novitiate. Reverend Mother came
to see her flock. The professed nun and the novice, the
oblate who was not there yesterday evening, and the
postulant, not forgetting 'Sister Piglet'. She asked me how
I had spent my first night in enclosure.

'Very well, Mother. I was dazzled by Matins. I never
thought it would be so beautiful.'

'Sister Bernadette isn't eating anything,' said Mother
Gertrude.

'That'll come later,' said Reverend Mother. 'You know
what they say? The vocation lies at the bottom of the
porringer . . .'

She added:

'Soon you must write to your brother, and give him your
news.'

She went out with Mother Gertrude. The novices bowed.
I followed Mother Emmanuelle into her office. Could I
speak to her for a moment? I wanted to read *Jésus en son
Temps*. I gave it to Mother Emmanuelle. The pages weren't
cut. I was ordered as regular reading (that is to say every day
after lunch) a preparation for the novitiate by Father
Rodriguez, general of the Jesuits in eighteen something or
other. It was easier to swallow than I expected.

Then I went for a long walk as far as the end of the
fields round the convent. I'd been given clogs, and I
couldn't keep up with Mother Gertrude's brisk pace.

Besides, she was big, and she went at a gallop. I lost my clogs, I limped on one foot, I made up for lost time, I stumbled and wanted to laugh. At last we burst out laughing, both of us. She took pity on me and slowed down. I came back exhausted, with my feet torn to ribbons.

My postulant's shoes seemed a delight to me after this martyrdom.

We were allowed to make the Stations of the Cross in the cloisters. Several nuns who met me embraced me, joyfully. As I didn't know any of them, I felt I was being embraced by a single habit with different faces. I let myself be kissed. After all, they couldn't have so many occasions to kiss postulants!

I went the round of the cloisters: the windows, which were closed, looked out on to a little lawn where, alas, there was a terrible statue of St. Joseph, the patron of our convent. He never has any luck, this saint, he is always shown as an old man. Why? Jesus just born, and Joseph a hundred years old? He must really have been a good-looking Jew of about thirty.

Inside the cloisters, the parquet was polished, and the Gothic windows were beautiful; but why were there so many horrible statues? The Stations of the Cross were not so ugly. In one corner there was a reproduction of the Holy Shroud of Turin. It was the first time I'd seen it. I couldn't take my eyes off it.

I learnt afterwards that we postulants and novices had no right to go into the cloisters, except on Sundays. I cast a final glance at the Holy Shroud and went up again to the novitiate as the bell for Vespers sounded. It was sung with the same solemnity as Matins. A full peal of bells was ringing.

Afterwards there was a meeting in Mother Emmanuelle's

office, with a distribution of sweets. We looked at one another rather like china dogs. Mother Emmanuelle guided the conversation very diplomatically. I learnt that 'Piglet' had already been a nun for twenty years and had taught somewhere in Alsace. One oblate came from the South of France. All three of us went and helped Mother Emmanuelle to finish a breviary.

We hadn't spoken much with Mother Emmanuelle, but the atmosphere had been friendly.

The same life must mould us all, unite us to the same end. What did we need to say to one another? In the evening, in the refectory, my throat was still constricted.

They sang the *Salve Regina*.

Such was my first day inside the convent.

7

The First Christmas

DAY succeeded day, with drawing, prayer, Offices, readings and walks. We had no recreation, only a long solitary walk. My dream was realized: we never spoke.

Sometimes Mother Emmanuelle or Mother Gertrude came in search of me, to give me advice or just to see if the silence wasn't too much for me. If only they could have known how I loved it! I had been such a chatterbox in the outside world, and now I found it so easy to be silent.

Signs took the place of words. I knew the signs that meant sleeping, eating, going out. I didn't manage to learn the others. The courses in the novitiate were sometimes very funny. Mother Emmanuelle asked us the meaning of a sign and, except for the young professed nun, we all sat like mutes. I must say that, except for Piglet, we always knew the other points of the Rule perfectly well. The novices were extremely nice and made me signs in slow motion. I stared at them . . . and didn't understand. Everyone was in fits of laughter.

We had singing lessons – I wasn't particularly bright – and lessons in dogma. The lessons in Holy Scripture were given by Father Luke. My school Latin came back to me; I even began to understand the psalms.

As a postulant, I was excused from Matins and got up rather late. In the morning I did a little housework; in the afternoon, we drew in a big room at the end of the building under Mother Gertrude's studio. We illustrated breviaries by making minute tracings of intricate arabesques down every page.

I should have liked to do it as skilfully as the monks of the Middle Ages. Piglet was not gifted, Sister Jeanne was adept, and I was between the two. But we were full of goodwill.

How anxious we were to do well!

Some time later came washing-day. General confusion. We put on thick aprons and clogs. The choir sisters and the lay sisters washed, wrung out, rubbed and rinsed, in a cloud of steam. We were delighted and intimidated to be with the community, particularly with the lay sisters, who were simple, open and gay. The Mothers felt they had to be more reserved. If my health had permitted it, I should certainly have been an extern. In a way it is easier, you only need to be able to work like a man; but alas! I can't.

The wash-house, at the far side of the courtyard, was enormous. The piles of linen were enough to dishearten the dead.

The sisters worked at a dizzy speed. What a job! I wondered how many years' practice you needed to reach that stage. Mother Gertrude didn't do too badly. The young lay sister had already got into the habit a bit; the big clothes-horse and Piglet and I were terrified. It was understood that a novice couldn't do very much, and a postulant could do even less. What would become of us? The externs watched us with amused benevolence. I threw myself into it and rubbed away so hard I almost took the skin off my fingers. I was no good.

Everything had been boiled already. In the stone tubs there were tuckers, socks, stockings, collars, underclothes, headbands, bonnets, and veils; white veils for the choir sisters, black for the Mothers and externs.

At half-time there was a distribution of bread-and-butter and jam and boiling coffee. By noon we were knocked up.

The Prioress was there: a big brown woman, with an authoritative voice and animated dark eyes. I was terrified of her. Luckily, Mother Gertrude looked after me. I rubbed, rubbed and rinsed till noon. They let us go a few minutes before Office, just in time to rush and change. I was soaked.

After the mid-day meal, I was so tired that Mother Gertrude excused me from going for a walk and sent me off to bed for an hour. I found a hot water bottle under the blankets and wept with gratitude. The bell rang for afternoon work. It seemed to me superhuman to get up.

A little later, Reverend Mother came to see me:

'Not too tired, Sister?'

'I'm holding out by praying like mad.'

The whole afternoon, mechanically, I said *Ave Maria*s. God be praised, the next washing day wouldn't be for another fortnight. My left hand was so swollen that I could hardly sleep at night. Luckily, I drew with my right hand.

Friday came, the day for Confession.

'Well,' asked Father Luke, 'how's it going? Not too cold?'

'No, I did the washing.'

He laughed, the wretch.

'Well . . . ?'

'I rubbed so hard that I can't use my left hand any more. Tomorrow I'm learning to sweep. Do you think I'll manage it?'

The clothes-horse, the oblate, Piglet and I had orders to sweep out the chapel, under the direction of Gertrude the mannequin. I loved going to the chapel. We began by dusting the walls with long feather-dusters, it was child's play. Then it grew harder, and got really tough. There we were, with our aprons, our soft-footed slippers and our brooms in our hands, at the heart of the convent.

I watched attentively to see how the sisters held their brooms. It wasn't as easy as it seemed. Mother Gertrude was a master of the broom, and wonderfully skilful. We swept in a line and pushed a heap of dust to a certain point, then we turned back again and brought up still more dust, thinner dust this time. And so on to the end of the choir. The aisles were swept in a masterly fashion by two sturdy externs.

Then Mother Gertrude tried to teach me to polish. It was a very comic lesson; she had to break it off so as not to lose her dignity. As for her, she polished away steadily, like a machine: forwards, backwards, and right to the middle of the parquet, with a speed that defied all competition. I always came in late myself, in spite of my efforts. And then I wasn't polishing at all. I pushed, I sweated, I rubbed, I danced, I did everything except polish, and finally, at the end of my strength, I burst out laughing.

The rest of the work was finished hell for leather. When the bell rang, we were exhausted, our hands and faces were black, our knees were knocking. We didn't understand much of the explanation of the next day's Office.

I had to pay attention all the same, because in a few weeks I should have to confess it publicly if I missed an anthem or a verse. We went to have a foot bath and change our clothes.

. . . . .

I loved Sunday in the convent. It was a real day of rest, joy and serenity. As if you took a great leap into oblivion. I used to go off on Sundays, myself, out into the country with God. I started the habit almost at once. I wanted to be alone. And there's only one way of being alone, isn't there? To go away. So I went away. Everything was plunged in complete and utter silence. It was incredible, the whole convent was listening to God.

I wrote to my brother: 'I'm very well, I'm so happy, everything's lovely here. Will you be coming at Christmas?'

Sunday . . . I understood my ardour, it was the only day when they gave us a breathing space. For the novitiate – I'm sorry: the postulancy – is exacting. They were so busy with me that I hadn't a minute now to think of God, I who had entered to think of God alone. It was a hard blow. When I complained to Father Luke, he answered:

'That'll be all right. Enter into your new life first, and the rest will follow.'

The week passed like lightning. There were so many rules and regulations, customs and new ways to learn that I almost went mad with them. I did my best and was subjected to enough instructions and advice to make a saint apprehensive. From time to time I gave vent to a wild gust of laughter. I tried in vain to suppress it, but it would burst out. The novitiate is gay. The community seemed to like me. And what about me? I never saw the same nun twice, but I loved every one of them, and all the more because they were strangers to me.

In the refectory I learnt how to fold my napkin the right way, but I didn't know how to cut the bread. The loaf was big, and the knife was small. Mother Gertrude helped me. I found it a little humiliating. I didn't always manage to swallow everything. As for the reading, I might as well have been in China.

We followed the season of Advent with fervour. For the first time in my life I prepared for the Coming of the Child.

It seemed that I was waiting for Him with Our Lady, going up to Bethlehem, filled with a secret happiness, for the census Herod had ordered.

. . . . .

On Christmas Eve, we went to bed at four in the afternoon, since we were singing Matins at nine that evening. We changed and put on our best habits before midnight Mass.

Oh, the arrival of the enclosed nuns at the chapel for the midnight Mass! Erect, majestic, their immaculate cloaks reaching down to the ground, their black veils with impeccable folds, their arms at their sides; they were no longer walking, they were flying, gliding, hieratic, withdrawn. They had left the earth.

We took our places in the stalls. I was somewhere in the back rows. The choirscreen opened on to the illuminated altar. There was a smell of flowers and incense. The feast was grave, mysterious and gay, all at the same time. My brother had sent the flowers round the tabernacle.

Father Luke celebrated Mass.

The convent was nothing now but a huge crib. With a single voice, a single heart, we sang, we had the honour of singing for the most beautiful feast in the world, the only one.

I wanted to be the ass in the stable, 'to breathe upon the Child', as the song says in its innocence, to look at Him eternally with wide and faithful eyes and lick His little feet with a great rough tongue. The eighty nuns turned towards Him, bowed, humbled themselves, prayed, went up to receive Holy Communion. We intoned Lauds: 'Let everything that has breath praise the Lord.' Then, for half an hour, the choir became a single silent and adoring presence.

There was a huge crib in the cloister, another in the chapel, one in the novitiate, one at the externs'. The Child is everywhere; He is born, He is born, He is born! And we know it! We are the witnesses.

In the refectory there was hot chocolate and a big cake for everyone.

You could only hear the clatter of spoons and cups being set down. But what joy there was in this silence! It burst out passionately. It shone through gesture, looks and gait, and even in the way we held up our heads. I was bursting with happiness and all the community was the same. I should have liked to take the whole world in my arms. No more disease, injustice, crime, stupidity, no more suffering or hunger. Dost Thou at least hearken unto me? Why so much happiness for me alone? What about them?

There were two telegrams on my plate: my brother was arriving on 1 January and a friend wished me a happy Christmas. That pleased me all the more since I wasn't expecting it.

It was cold. I drank my chocolate and went up to the dormitory.

I looked very well – as rosy-cheeked as an apple – when my brother came. We chatted and laughed. Reverend Mother came into the parlour for a minute. The atmosphere was friendly. I had prayed so hard that the fact of seeing me behind a grille should not give him pain.

.   .   .   .   .

Life went on. The knot in my throat at meals relaxed a little. I was able to eat a little, but I had grown considerably thinner.

The convent had flu . . . one by one the sisters vanished

from the choir and the refectory. Soon we were reduced to a third of the community. There were distributions of pills and grogs: it seemed that nothing would stop this epidemic. Though Lent had begun, there were eggs and pancakes in the refectory, and dishes made with butter.

Nearly all the externs had to take to their beds. Then came the turn of the Mothers, and then the novitiate, the young lay sister, Piglet, the oblate. Reverend Mother held out, on the strength of pills. She was hoarse, coughing heavily, and wrapped up in a black shawl, but she continued to preside over all the Offices.

The laundry was a great burden. It took us two days to do. The first evening I was so tired that I was excused from going back to it. But rather than stay in the icy dormitory I decided to try once again. I didn't rub very much. I had such a migraine and I felt so ill that everything was swimming. I went in search of Mother Emmanuelle who gave me two pills, and advised me not to take them, it was a question of mortifying one's body. I found that rather hard to understand, but hadn't I come here to understand such things? I didn't take the pills.

When we had had the last Benediction after Compline, I don't know how I reached my bed.

Next day, I joined the flock of invalids in the infirmary dormitory. I felt such bliss when I found myself in a warm place that I wanted to go on having flu all the winter. Later, my better feelings returned to me.

I was looked after and purged so energetically that I was soon quite empty. We drank hot drinks by the pint; the fever fell rapidly, but I was as weak as a new-born child. So was everyone else, for that matter. To my astonishment, the community was given a whole month's rest. We went to bed after Vespers, that is to say at four, and we rose at five in the morning for early Mass, then we went up again to sleep a little longer. I got back some of my strength. We were given sugar: five lumps a day.

When I asked Reverend Mother the reason for the month's rest, she answered:

'Our life is hard, it is wearing, tiredness accumulates. This rest was necessary, people's health is not what it was before the war.'

Gradually the community was restored to health.

They even served us with enormous *quiches lorraines*. I wanted to laugh. The whole situation seemed amusing to me.

Then the novices began to work again. We scraped the vegetables near a radiator. When they thought we had warmed up enough, we returned to our drawing.

We went back to the dormitory. It was the first of March. The cold was bearable. Only Mother Gertrude prolonged her stay in the infirmary by order of Reverend Mother. I learned that she suffered terribly from insomnia.

The worst was over. Already the earth smelt good. The sun tried to shine through. Another month and it would be mild. I counted the nights, then I felt that was mean and I didn't think about it any more.

When the breviary we had been working on was finished, they changed my occupation and I was sent to the work-room with Mother Gertrude. She was gay, intelligent and greatly loved; she got through a fantastic amount of work. One never saw her waste time.

Since the sale of our cheese was no longer enough to support the convent, some benefactors had suggested that the enclosed nuns should open a workroom to make coffin-fittings: nylon pillows and mattresses. In spite of this funereal occupation, the workroom was very gay. You forgot what these under-mattresses and cushions were to be used for, there were luxurious ones in mauve nylon, with lace; most of them were white. All were sewn by machine. One day I tried out an outfit, as I was the thinnest. It was the joke of the morning.

My first job was to unfold and glue enormous cardboard boxes which were used for packing up the pillows and mattresses. When the orders were urgent, Mother Gertrude and the lay sisters sat up very late. One or two evenings we were allowed to work with them. It was a cause of pride to me. There was hot tea and cream tarts. On those nights, we only slept for two hours.

The workroom, at the far end of the dormitory, was full of light. The big windows looked out on one side on to the convent courtyard, and on the other, they overlooked the farmyard. The first time I had to seal the boxes with four large strips of gummed paper, I thought I should never be able to manage it. And to think it seemed so easy to me afterwards! But I shall remember those beginnings with Mother Françoise, under the amused observation of Mother Gertrude. I later became very good at the job and managed to glue up about twenty boxes every morning and another twenty every afternoon. I was, in fact, the wrapper-up of coffin mattresses. Postulant, singer and gluer-up of cardboard boxes, all at the Trappistine convent. Who could say that God hasn't got a sense of humour?

When the boxes piled up too much, I worked on the floor below, where I had painted the breviary. It wasn't heated. In vain I dipped my hands into boiling water to stick the strips of paper, I was weeping with cold and my numb blue hands no longer obeyed me. One particularly painful morning, just when I was going up again, I caught Mother Gertrude's glance. My eyes were still red. She didn't say anything, but after that I didn't have to go down there again.

One Sunday, when Mother Gertrude was still in the infirmary dormitory, I had permission to go and see her.

'I am four months old today.'

As I hadn't the right to speak any more, I explained myself by signs. She didn't understand.

'Four days?' she asked. 'Four years? Forty years?'

I laughed and said again, if you can express it that way: 'No, four months.'

I added:

'I have just been born. I entered the Trappistine convent on 1 November. So I was born on 1 November. Today is 1 March, so I am four months old.' She smiled.

During the flu epidemic that felled the convent, Father Luke had brought Communion to those who were kept in bed with high fever. I can't remember why, but one afternoon he came into the infirmary dormitory. He passed in front of my alcove as I was drinking a cup of tea, and he said to me:

'You look like a grandmother, with your postulant's bonnet.'

I never saw him again.

8

Holy Week

APART from the Sunday morning sermon, which was always extremely short, we attended a course in Church history or an explanation of Scriptures every Thursday. One week, this course was replaced by a meeting of the community in the chapter on Saturday.

The grille opened and Father Maur – the new chaplain – appeared before the nuns: pale, bloodless features, a bony face and a metallic voice. He bid us welcome, put himself entirely at our disposal – he would be in the confessional every day between six and seven for anyone who wanted him – but, whatever happened, no one must come and complain of this or that, he would always side with the superiors.

I was astonished to hear what he said. Complain? But what about?

He added:

'Father Luke was your confessor for six years. In principle, a confessor should only stay three years. He may stay on another three if the community wants him. But after that, according to canon law, he can return to his monastery.'

So Father Luke had gone back to his monastery. I rejoiced for him.

Father Maur had been in the Order for thirty-five years.

So he knew our life and customs, our joys and problems. In spite of his austere appearance, I was not afraid of him. on the contrary.

He assured us again he was at our service and the chapter grille was closed. The community withdrew.

My first conversations with the priest who would be my spiritual father were brief. With a single word he guided me, steadied my steps, disciplined my joy and my relations with God. I hid nothing from him. Thanks to him I began my apprenticeship.

From time to time Mother Emmanuelle summoned me to her office. I still recall her tenderness and intelligence. Once a month we were called to see Reverend Mother. The whole community went to her in turn; first the professed nuns, the oldest, then the novices and the lay sisters. I was the last, I followed Piglet, who had entered a few weeks before me.

The first time I was summoned, I waited half an hour. Knowing that I was going to speak to Christ's representative (for this was the place Reverend Mother held in the convent), I knelt trembling in front of her door. In fact, I felt as sick inside as if I was taking my *baccalauréat*. When my turn came, I couldn't utter. My throat was constricted, my heart was beating as I gazed at Reverend Mother: the living incarnation of religious life.

She put me at ease:

'It's a fine thing to be a postulant, I envy you.'

She added gaily:

'No, I don't, because I've done half the journey already.' (She had been a professed nun for more than twenty-five years.)

We never had any 'spiritual conversation'. Never a single word about this mysterious life that had been hers for so long. On my second visit, she asked me how I was getting on.

'I'm having great difficulty with the manual work. I'm not as quick as our Sisters. I'm tired after the Saturday cleaning,' I told her.

'You will get used to it,' she answered. 'In my time, we swilled out the chapel, it was hard work. I've often done it. I'm not so strong now, I'm getting old.'

She was activity itself; and I smiled when she added, like a good housewife:

'Now the floors are polished, it's easier.'

I was still thirsty. But if I learnt no secret of spiritual life, I came out refreshed and, if possible, even gayer from these brief interviews.

.   .   .   .   .

So life unrolled itself, as uniform as a ribbon. I tried to absorb the Holy Rule, I followed it, read it, studied it, thought it, swallowed it, I just about managed not to eat it. A living Rule; I had to become a living Rule. There was much to be done before I achieved it. I walked too fast, all my movements were too abrupt. I was impatient, I looked as if I knew everything, whereas in fact I forgot everything I was told: I had the brain of a linnet.

As a rule, the postulants were given charge of the harmonium books. I was so in the clouds that they postponed my initiation into these functions. As you had to go and prostrate yourself every time you made a mistake, I ran a strong risk of spending Office flat on my face in front of the screen.

I was always very glad to meet Reverend Mother in the corridor or to catch a glimpse of her when she passed like a whirlwind on her way to the novitiate or the workroom.

The time of remorse was over, I was walking gaily in the right path; my victories were gifts from God; my defeats taught me to know myself. In spite of my pride, my cowardice, my fear of effort and sacrifice, I knew that with God I was capable of everything.

Father Maur guided me forcefully. One could sense the kindness underneath his austerity. Every day brought me new riches. The secret life of the friends of God was opening to me.

I had a dream, I don't think it was imagination, it was too clear. The impression I felt was so strong I remained quite shaken by it.

One evening, in the dormitory, I fell asleep praying as usual, perhaps with more fervour than usual. My prayer went on, I no longer knew where I was. I was thinking of those words of Jesus to Peter:

'Dost thou love Me?'

I saw the scene, the radiant apparition that asked for love from His friend, but it was no longer from His friend, it was from me He asked it.

Within myself, with all my faith, with all my tenderness, I murmured very gently, so as not to wake anyone, above all not Mother Gertrude who slept so lightly:

'Yes, I love Thee.'

The question was repeated emphatically several times as if by someone who needed reassurance.

And I, in turn, repeated:

'Yes, I love Thee, I love Thee, I love Thee . . .'

I was overwhelmed, sobbing with love, emotion and contrition, and I continued to swear that I loved Him.

The bell for Matins was sounding. I arrived at early Mass, my face swollen with tears.

At breakfast I was still crying for joy. I couldn't stop. During work, there were still a few tears on my cheeks.

'Sister Bernadette hasn't slept much,' Mother Gertrude said kindly.

I smiled:

'It's nothing.'

A little later, Reverend Mother came to look round the workroom. I was checking the pillows. She sent for me:

'Mother Gertrude tells me that you were sobbing all night. Are you ill?'

'No, Mother, I'm very well.'

Silence. She looked at me. I said:

'They were tears of happiness.'

I hesitated. Must I confess my secret? I remembered that nothing should be hidden from superiors, and I took my courage in both hands:

'Mother, do you want to know why?'

'As you like.'

I told her about my marvellous dream.

She looked quizzical, and teased me:

'No one said to you: "Feed My sheep"?'

'Mother, don't you believe me?'

'But of course, of course . . .'

I was sorry that I had told her. Dream or impression, I was not asleep, that was certain. So it couldn't have been imagination. Was it wrong to weep for love, affection and emotion? Why?

I decided that I would only confide in my confessor.

On Friday I told him what had happened and what I had decided.

'You aren't absolutely bound to unveil the workings of your heart, even to me. You have such freedom as far as this goes that if you wanted to confess to another monk or to the village curé, you could demand it.' I laughed:

'I don't intend to.'

'It's only to show you how free you are.'

The first fortnight, I had had the right to talk to Mother Gertrude. After this, she continued to speak to me but I had to answer her by signs. It was very comic. Happily I improvised a sort of personal language with head and eyes and hands and managed to make myself understood. We were allowed to speak to answer Reverend Mother, or the Mistress of Novices, and, during lessons, we could speak about the subject in question.

I was very glad of this silence; it made our freedom complete. What a paradox!

The community was gay, animated and kind. I lived in silence with eighty friends around me. Out in the world, who could boast as much? The same life, the same occupations, the same use of time, the same goal, everything drew us together. I let myself be borne along by the community.

One morning, Reverend Mother stopped me as I passed: it was exactly five and a half months since I had been enclosed.

'Don't you want to take the veil?'

Seeing me stupefied and speechless, she went on:

'You will take the veil of an oblate on Easter Night. That's what comes of being good.'

Had I really been good?

She saw I was startled, and she gave me a friendly little wink and disappeared. I thought to myself: 'As a rule, you need six months as a postulant, but I have waited three months at the door. I shall have a white serge robe, like the others. I've finished with this grandmother's garb. I shall pass unnoticed. I shall be Thine, whatever the colour or cloth of my habit. I shall stay here all my life. I am going to have every minute of every hour. Every gesture I make, even the most ordinary, even the humblest, will be a declaration of love. They are going to shave my head as a sign of renunciation. I am going to become a real nun.'

   .   .   .   .   .

Lent was not strict that year. The flu epidemic had been so severe that they were taking care of us.

'In my time,' said Mother Emmanuelle, 'Lent was stricter: we got up at two in the morning, sang Matins, went down to Mass and didn't have coffee till six. The first meal was at one. I thought several times I should faint with hunger. The stove was lit in the morning from nine to eleven, then they put it out. Reverend Mother was the Mistress of Novices at the time. Her office was warmer, so she left the door ajar to give the novitiate a little warmth. As she caught pneumonia as a result, the Visiting Father ordered her to sleep in her study after that, and not in the dormitory.'

All these privations had undermined Mother Emmanuelle's poor health, and she was obliged to abandon her post of Mistress of Novices. Mother Aleth, the young professed nun who had known her since her arrival, was weeping.

I felt no remorse for my indifference—I am here for God, I thought, let Him give us Mother X or Mother Y, what does it matter, as long as you obey?

The Prioress, the big authoritative brunette, succeeded Mother Emmanuelle as Mistress of Novices. She combined both functions. Again, I noticed her fine dark eyes, and her brusque manners. I was a little afraid of her.

'I will get used to it,' I thought, 'it's a question of will-power. I must.'

With repeated Hail Marys I had certainly come to put up with the stupidity of Piglet, the curiosity of Mother Aleth. I used the same remedy to calm my fears.

.   .   .   .   .

Lent was drawing to its close.

Holy Week began. Through the readings in the refectory, in the cloister, in the sermons of Father Maur and the conversations in the novitiate, we were witnesses of the plot of the Sanhedrin, of the betrayal, and we shared the fear of His friends. The Cistercian liturgy is beautiful, we not only followed Offices, we lived them.

From Wednesday onwards we didn't *chant*, we *said* the psalms, except that the professed nuns intoned the lamentations as recitations. It was strange and moving. You would have thought them mourners. The Gregorian chant, by its simple purity, lends itself to sadness. For three days we lamented God Who died.

In the refectory there was only one meal a day, with one course; in the evening, a stew, in the morning, black coffee with a minute piece of bread. Can one eat when Jesus dies?

The convent was just a breath of love suspended in the steps of the Son of Man, day by day, hour by hour, and, at the end, minute by minute.

On the Wednesday, He spoke for the last time to the Jews under the portals of the Temple.

From Holy Thursday onwards, the choristers hardly did any of their usual work. The Offices were very long. I found it hard to keep standing. We were hungry.

On Thursday night I couldn't sleep. That night, surrounded by His friends, knowing that He was going to die for them, trembling with fear, distraught with love, He made us the ultimate gift.

I should have liked to prostrate myself on the ground all night, to go into a hole and hide there. To burrow down in adoration. But the Rule forbids us to leave our beds.

The atmosphere of Good Friday was unforgettable.

Deep silence reigned. We went about quietly. A single thought within our eighty heads.

The altar was quite bare without Him. There was an altar of repose in the chapter-house. We were in mourning. Even the regulation cup of coffee was no longer passed to anyone.

At three o'clock, in the choir, we prostrated ourselves, face against the floor. We held lighted candles that we extinguished at the moment of His death.

At noon, we had bread and water. The oldest professed nun read the Gospel according to St. John. It is the most beautiful of all. I knew that chapter by heart, followed every word she read with my lips, memory and heart.

Vespers and Office of the Dead. We prayed for the whole of the world. That Friday, after Matins, the whole dormitory gave themselves the discipline. I was dying of jealousy not to be able to do it too. The honour of discipline is reserved for the professed nuns. The weak are exempt. Mentally, Lord, I kick myself without mercy for all the sins and stupidities of my life. Forgive me. I promise I will change.

Tomorrow I take the veil.

.   .   .   .   .

As an exception, I was allowed to have a real bath. The Rule favoured showers.

It wasn't unpleasant, a hot bath. In fact, I was rather worried by the pleasure it gave me. I washed myself as fast as I could to mortify myself, and the hot water scalded me. I saw how thin I was. 'I am not giving You a fine gift.'

They shaved my head.

The Prioress made me try on my robe. As it was all billowing, she said in a rough, friendly way:

'Got to fill all that up, Sister Bernadette.'

(I hope Thou dost not prefer plump women!)

My weariness is terrible, but joy is like a prop; so I am still standing.

On Saturday Thou wert still dead. We read about the visit that Peter made to Thy tomb. John ran faster, saw Thou wert there no more. The angels had neatly folded the linen. Before, at dawn, Magdalen had come. Thou wert awaiting Magdalen in the garden, and she was greatly moved, and did not know Thee. There was a reason for it. She had lost her head. I am already losing mine, myself, here where I do not see Thee. What should I have felt in Thy time?

9

The Taking of the Veil

EASTER. We spent our time the same way as at Christmas: at four o'clock a collation with dried fruit, nuts and jam. We rested till Matins, which we chanted with all our hearts about nine in the evening. He is come again. The Gregorian text was bold. *Resurrexi . . . et adhuc sum tecum,* so it made Christ say when He spoke to His Father.

And then, and then, I should have liked to write it in letters of gold, of fire, in some indelible way, AND THEN I put on my habit as an oblate.

The Prioress helped me to put the coif on my shaven head, the band around my forehead, kept in place with a pin, the white wimple round my shoulders. I was so exhausted I couldn't hold anything. The Prioress got to work with alarming speed; as for me, I dropped the pins and trembled. The wimple gripped my head, compressed my face, it was terribly uncomfortable. I felt myself becoming a mummy. I felt ridiculous. What a pity! To love You and to have to be dressed up like that! It all made me awkward. I would rather have been bareheaded.

I was cold in the long billowing chemise with its sleeves caught in at the wrists. I felt trussed up in the white robe and heavy cloak, rather like a sweet wrapped up in sticky paper. There I was, dressed as You had asked. I was content and at the same time rather unhappy.

The Prioress dressed me with her usual energy. I was led

to Reverend Mother who hastily blessed me. That was my taking of the veil. Quick, quick, let's go and hide in a little corner! I delight in it – but I am a little humiliated. 'You marry me without documents. Don't lovers have the finest jewels? You know my distress, you know I have nothing to give You. I am poor. I am marrying well.'

.   .   .   .   .

I had been terrified to hear accounts of a novice taking the veil. She was dressed as a bride, and kissed her family for the last time in the hall of the chapter-house. Then there was a procession out of the convent, led by the bishop. He knocked three times at the enclosure door with his crosier. The door was opened and the novice was admitted into the precincts from which the procession continued to the chapel. The novice prostrated herself, and asked to be received into the Order. They burnt a lock of her hair. She was dead to the world. Yes, a moving ceremony, but very painful for her near relations. And so I'd much rather have everything happen inside the convent. I had not left the theatre to find it again.

I went into the chapel that Paschal night, walking last, feeling nervous in my white habit. One lamp lit the choir. It was put out as soon as the nuns had reached their places. Father Maur, alone, held a lighted candle.

We sang *Lumen Christi*, three times, each time more loudly. The Paschal candle was lit. It weighed five kilos, I had never seen such a big one. Then we lit our candles and the Easter Mass began. My nuptial Mass.

What a pity that I sing out of tune. Why didst Thou not make me a bird?

I understood what she must be feeling, the extern whose

golden wedding would soon be celebrated. She was baptised, confirmed, and took the veil on Easter night. She wore the white baptismal robe for a week. May I keep mine for always. May Thy hands alone take it from me the day of my death. On the Day of Judgement, I shall see what I believe. Alleluia . . . sang the choir, confirming my joy. To extol Thee here all my life is indeed the noblest, finest occupation, the occupation most deserving praise. To sing out of tune, but to sing all the same.

Thou hast taught me much during these few months, but it is not enough. My life is beginning. I am listening . . . Only today I make my first appearance as an oblate.

After Mass and Matins we went to drink the traditional hot chocolate and eat our piece of brioche. There was some mail beside my plate: my brother was coming this summer. Two letters from friends, and one of them called me a coward.

Coward? What did that mean?

I was going to sleep fully dressed like a real enclosed nun. I took off the wimple, the veil and the day band and put on the wimple, the veil and the band worn at night. I put my head on the pillow. I felt like a giant compress. I hoped that that would pass.

I had a slight migraine. I stretched myself out dutifully on the mattress. I crossed my hands on my breast and went to sleep. The night smelt good: whiffs of budding trees came in through the window. Soon the flowers would be coming out. There were buds everywhere. The days were growing longer. We should end by going to bed in broad daylight.

At Matins, the birds were singing at the tops of their voices. In the refectory they came and squabbled under our noses.

I was now entrusted with the harmonium books. I often made mistakes, but luckily Mother organist had been playing for twenty years; she never made mistakes, whatever score I put in front of her.

Once, when I was particularly lost in the clouds – it was nearly summer time – I gave her a canticle for Lent. She was so surprised and pulled such a face that we burst into uncontrollable laughter. I was preparing to go and prostrate myself when Reverend Mother made a sign and excused me from it.

Daniel-Rops' *Jésus en son Temps* had been given back to me, and I read it, with the Gospel of St. Luke, every day, two or three lines a day. I had never till then read in such small doses. It was an excellent idea, you remembered better and thought about what you were reading. At first I used to say to myself: 'It's no use reading two lines.' I even learnt to do it very slowly. Every word sank into my mind and stayed there.

I had a hard and repulsive job apart from the job in the workroom: once a week it was my job to clean out the lavatories. The first few times, especially, I wanted to cry, I really think I was weak enough to shed a tear or two. Later I got so used to it that I was almost sorry when my work was changed.

Downstairs there was a room they called the 'cloak room'. That was where shawls and cloaks and aprons hung. In the cupboard were straw hats and clogs. One door opened into the garden, the other into a corridor that led to the lavatories. I detested them. I was terribly afraid of them. They were damp. My first impression was terrifying. I followed the young professed nun or Mother Gertrude, who was to show me how to work, as if I was going to the galleys. You had to clean them out once a week. You had to wash the very primitive wooden seats with boiling water. Phew! There were seven lavatories, in the seventh there were two buckets and lots and lots of spiders' webs; that was the one I was most afraid of.

In the workroom Mother Gertrude made the work seem like recreation. Infectious good humour reigned there. And yet Mother Gertrude rather disappointed me. One high feast day, in the afternoon, just when we were putting on our aprons and our work-sleeves, Sister Jeanne the oblate, the young professed nun and the clothes-horse took the book of 'Us' (the usages and customs of the convent) and, for a joke, showed me the chapter where it was written:

'On feast days, the enclosed nuns will be exempted from manual work so that they can completely devote themselves to the thought of God.'

They wanted to show it to Mother Gertrude for fun. They took the book, but when they got to the workroom they didn't dare: they laughed, and begged me to do it. I innocently went up to the ladder where Mother Gertrude was perching and showed her the passage, she laughed even louder than we did.

A few days later I passed Reverend Mother, who said to me very gently, with a look of amusement:

'Oh yes, Sister Bernadette, on feast days *too*!'

I racked my brains to understand what she meant, she bent over me as I knelt down:

'There might, there might perhaps . . . be some dispute about the Rule? . . .'

She was tactful enough not to finish. I thought it unnecessary to explain such a trifle. In future, I would not joke with Mother Gertrude.

The weather began to be mild. The cloister garden was

full of roses. The sun shone brightly through the novitiate windows.

At meals, we had salad and fruit. Summer comes rapidly in the Vosges. It is short and stormy.

When there was a big order in the workroom, everyone worked without respite. I wrapped up, glued and labelled. The cardboard boxes full of mattresses or pillows were sent down through an opening into the courtyard where Robert, the big red-faced man, and Jean, our workman, put them into the cheese van. Piglet had carried something that was too heavy for her, and she became ill and feverish. They put her into the infirmary: that was one place I hoped I should never set foot in. There were great heat-waves as the summer drew on. We were given light serge habits.

We went gooseberry-picking: in clogs and straw hats, with baskets under our arms, we set out in single file for the orchard. I was the last by a long way, the clogs still hindered me terribly. There were little bushes covered with red and white gooseberries, planted alternately, one red, one white: we attacked the red. We crouched down and picked rapidly. The heat was stifling, we were streaming with sweat. During the afternoon's picking we were allowed to have a break and sit down on the grass. What with our big straw hats and our snack, I could believe myself on the other side, unenclosed, with Sister Marie-Joseph. When the Prioress was there, she talked. The old professed nuns were allowed to speak if they asked permission; they didn't abuse it. The conversation reminded me of Camille and Madeleine in the tales of Ségur.

My happiness was boundless, but I was very tired physically. Mother Gertrude noticed it and warned Reverend Mother. They put me on a fattening diet. What a horrible word! And, finally, in the infirmary refectory, where you ate meat, fish, and eggs done in cream. There was a loud-speaker for transmitting the reading from the refectory. You felt a little like someone infected with the plague, cut off from the rest of the community.

St. Benedict knew what he was imposing when he ordered the recalcitrant monk to be parted from his community and take his meals alone. If the disobedience was more serious, the separation was made complete.

To be in the infirmary refectory, even for my health, seemed a penance to me. And a slight humiliation. Community life is so gay.

I suppose that the winter cold, and fatigue, had given me a pretty violent attack of colitis: I had burnings in my intestines and constantly felt sick.

The doctor from the neighbouring town – he was a proper vet – didn't understand it at all. So, after a shower and a change of clothes, they sent me into the town with Mother Emmanuelle, who was still feverish, Mother Françoise, and Piglet, all in charge of the Prioress. Under her vigilant guard, I saw a surgeon, a friend of the community. He decided that I needed a small operation. While the others were waiting, I went into a church nearby. They were baptizing an adult. I really suffered by coming out of the convent. In spite of our black cloaks, people looked at us. That didn't matter to me. But I had not left the world, left Paris and Nancy, to go back to it, even for my health. What did an attack of colitis matter?

'Whatever disturbs my conversation with God makes me suffer. Quick, quick, back to the cloister, let me regain my calm and the atmosphere of prayer. I wonder how I could have existed before?'

As we went back in the cheese van, I felt a general sigh of relief. I'm sure that we were all feeling the same, especi-

ally the professed nuns who had not put their noses outside
for twenty years.

They didn't say any more about my health. And, as they
didn't, I imagined that the doctor wouldn't do anything.
The burnings went on. I even found it hard to sit for any
length of time. My brother came to see me. He thought I
looked very well indeed. The colitis germs were evidently
well brought up and didn't make their appearance on your
face. Georges brought me the life of St. Bernadette, by
Michel de Saint-Pierre.

After my brother had gone, Reverend Mother announced
to me:

'You are to go into the clinic in three weeks.'

I thought: 'Even if it were a more serious operation,
like cutting off my leg, I couldn't say anything. Submission,
total submission to the will of God, manifested through the
superiors. That can go a long way.'

I was very sad to leave the convent: but off I went with a
charming little extern, the size of a mouse. Robert drove us
to Nancy.

A week later I was back. The sisters in the clinic had
received me as if I were a saint . . . And all because the
Trappistines are considered the most austere Order. What
difference can that make? That isn't sanctity.

When I had thanked the matron and sisters who had
spoilt me so, I climbed into the cheese van. The journey was a
little wearing. I was very tired, my back was hurting me. For
the last few miles, I thought I was going to faint.

It was dark, the van went through the village, and
through the big gate into the inner courtyard of the convent. How silent it was! Even in a clinic kept by nuns,
there was no silence to compare with ours.

Everything was quiet, everything was marvellously calm

and serene. Yes, God, it is indeed in the depths of a heart prepared by eternal silence that Thou art found.

I got out of the van and bumped into Reverend Mother. She dragged me off to the infirmary, to the room where Sister Marie-Raymond was sleeping. I knelt at Reverend Mother's feet as she waited, anxiously, for news:

'I'm all right. The little lay sister has to stay another few days at the clinic.'

I stayed a month in the infirmary. Why so long? I said nothing. I was so glad to be back. Everyone was at the reading before Compline. I went to the refectory. I wasn't hungry, since I had eaten a good deal at the clinic. The sisters must have thought that we Trappistines were starving, for they literally crammed me. I was alone in the silent, dark refectory. They had left the kitchen door open. A ray of light came through to me; and, through the loudspeaker, I heard the reader's voice. I had found that unreal, mysterious atmosphere again. I was at home again. 'Outside the convent, Thou are not the same, I cannot concentrate, too many outward things divide me from Thee. The source is here. Let this small test be salutary to me, and make me understand the vanity of the world.'

I had a bad night, my first night in the infirmary.

Little by little, I grew stronger, and a month later I was up to the mark again. What a joy it was to go back to the icy dormitory!

.   .   .   .   .

Custom demands that every year the convent should be inspected by a priest, who is named by the chapter-general of the Order which meets annually at Cîteaux. This Visiting Father has the right to enter the enclosure and to see all the buildings. He receives each nun individually in the parlour. After this a solemn session is held in the chapter-house. The novices and professed nuns are excluded from it. There he drafts a note criticizing the convent, or giving encouragement if there is reason for it. This judgment remains a secret. There is a public assembly before his departure, and the whole convent is summoned to it.

A few days before the Visiting Father's arrival, we had a monster spring cleaning, from the attics to the hen-houses by way of the refectory, and the dormitory where the mattresses were emptied, cleaned, and re-stuffed. The walls of each cubicle, the wooden bedsteads, everything was washed.

We had mown the lawns in the big main courtyard. The novitiate pulled up the weeds, and raked and swept the paths. The convent floors were swilled down. Everyone took part and even so there weren't too many of us. This exhausting work was done with good humour and incredible speed. Reverend Mother supervised her troops, and lent a hand. Washing the dormitory was hard work. So was carrying the mattresses into the courtyard. There was a great profusion of drinks: coffee (synthetic, but hot), wine, and orangeade.

When the Visiting Father arrived, a special peal of bells rang out and the whole convent was in a flutter.

.   .   .   .   .

Then came All Saints' Day again, and Christmas. Such was my first year with the Trappistines.

10

Our Daily Life

IN the summer we went to bed at eight instead of seven, but we had an hour's siesta. It was so close that we fell asleep heavily. It was hard to get up. It took me a good five minutes before I could follow Office except with my lips and by force of habit.

If you couldn't sleep in this hour of rest, you were allowed to read. For the tenth time I began the account of Bernadette's visions. Alas, I regularly went to sleep after two pages.

When I finally reached the account of the first vision, I had to stop, I was choking with emotion. Later I read it again. The words burnt me, engraved themselves on my memory. Sometimes I repeated them quickly to myself during a walk or in the corridors. Every time I relived the scene with such intensity that I bumped into the walls.

. . . I used to murmur the words of Bernadette:

'A young girl of sixteen to seventeen, clad in white, a yellow rose at her feet, holding a golden rosary . . .'

I began to learn: I now knew in detail all the events in the life of Christ. I had not only read and re-read the Gospels. I had read and re-read the commentaries, too. I always came back to my favourite: St. John. I knew several chapters of it by heart, especially the ones about the Passion and the Resurrection. A few words were enough to enrapture me.

.　　.　　.　　.　　.

Once a week, there was a meeting in the novitiate.

The Prioress asked:

'What have you got to say against Sister Bernadette?'

Every time I was in a cold sweat.

If no one moved, the Prioress could accuse me herself. If a sister rose, I had to prostrate myself in front of my seat.

Then the Prioress would say to me:

'Rise, in the name of the Lord.'

I would rise, and go and kneel down in the middle of the novitiate.

I heard the fault denounced. I prostrated myself again in sign of repentance and waited for the penance: usually a prayer for the person who had accused you, so that there should be no feeling of temper or rancour in us.

If the criticism was inaccurate or exaggerated, so much the worse for one's pride.

Sometimes, on the advice of the Mistress of Novices, we accused ourselves. Sometimes, too, we all accused ourselves of the same fault, and the whole novitiate lay on the ground to rise again quickly on the orders of the Prioress.

The accusations were made so tactfully that even the most susceptible could not criticize them:

'No doubt our little sister has forgotten . . .'

The number of times that I had forgotten was in fact incalculable: I forgot everything . . . and I still walked too fast. The young professed nun, Mother Aleth, accused me with all her might. I was beginning to find it amusing. I don't believe she always had a reason.

I was grateful for it later, for she had done me a service. It isn't pleasant to correct a sister. We were advised not to accuse a sister we disliked, but to pray for her.

One morning, as I was shutting the windows of the novitiate, I caught sight of myself in the glass. Instead of drawing away as the Rule recommends, I went up closer. I accused myself of it to the Prioress; she condemned me to go round the refectory looking at myself in a pocket mirror.

I blushed as I passed Reverend Mother's table; she pretended not to see me, so did all the Mothers and Sisters, except one who wanted to laugh. So I looked at myself attentively as I passed each Sister: I looked like a white cheese. They made me a sign to stop, or I should have spent the whole of lunch doing it.

Penances were made in the refectory. If you had broken something, you stayed kneeling at the door while the community was going in. Or you drank your soup on a little bench in the middle of the room. After the *Benedicite* the sisters who had to accuse themselves went down on their knees one behind the other, and reproached themselves one by one, for making unnecessary signs, for being late, for not following the whole Office.

At first I used to be horrified. I was very much afraid I should have to accuse myself. Later, I was completely indifferent. In Lent you asked to be allowed to mortify yourself by prostrating yourself at the exit of the chapel or the refectory so that the community should pass over you. You had to do so in great humility. I don't think I succeeded. The last sister to pass gave you a slight tap to tell you it was over.

The penances were performed with such spirit and submission that they seemed like a game. For a long time I was taken in. It was only much later I understood that it wasn't so easy to discard your pride in doing well or drawing attention to yourself. St. Bernard assures us that this sin will die a quarter of an hour after we do.

I had grown silent, I no longer moved my lips in order to

answer. When someone talked to me, I didn't know the signs well, but I made no useless ones, so to speak. Under Father Maur's energetic guidance, I was occupied exclusively with God. I saw nothing else. I knew nothing else. I tried to love Him.

I was very fond of the Prioress, she showed uncommon patience and kindness where I was concerned. She never grumbled at me or took the slightest notice of my clumsiness. Nor did anyone else, for that matter. Once, however, when I used the wrong tub at the washing, I saw an extern, red with fury, looking as if she could murder me. It's true that I wasn't much help to her. I watched her grow angry with curiosity. And with a certain fear. Suppose she was going to kill me? I should be dead, deceased, a martyr of the wash. How glorious! And so I watched her shake, her lips became convulsed, her face grew crimson. I was just thinking she would burst, when with a furious gesture she pushed me away and seized the tub. Slightly embarrassed, but determined not to give in in front of someone new, she began to laugh. So did I, and that was the end of the story.

One morning, I didn't hear the bell for getting up, or the bell for early Mass, or even the bell for Chapter. No one noticed my absence. At early Mass, the novices thought I was ill. At breakfast, Mother Gertrude, seeing I was not next to her, set off in search of me and found me fast asleep.

I took Communion all alone at High Mass, which scared me a good deal.

'Sleeping well is the sign of a sure vocation,' said Reverend Mother, teasing me. 'The same thing happened to me when I was a postulant.'

I seemed to be able to follow our life, though there were moments of difficulty. I had fits of giddiness, and migraines, I was hungry, sleepy, my mind was dull and not quick off the mark any more. The last week in Lent, the Sisters grew pale, staggered and fainted; but they smiled and laughed and forgot about it.

I forgot all these troubles in the chapel. There the hours passed like seconds. My love gave me strength.

On Sundays, when I wasn't in the country, I was in the choir, kneeling in my stall, alone in a corner with God. I said loving things to Him. Then I was silent. I looked at Him. Then I listened to Him. I saw an inner light: you had to close your eyes to see it. I was attaining Him, understanding Him with the spirit. I was losing the notion of my surroundings: I no longer existed. I could have stayed there all my life.

I waited for Sundays more and more impatiently.

.   .   .   .   .

Easter, nocturnal Communion, joyful chants, sweet-smelling nights, growing flowers . . . Happily I continued my second year at the Convent. I had learnt to know the animals. We had been to see a little calf, only a day old. The lay sister who looked after it was as proud of it as if she had been the cow. Then there were the pigs. What a horror they were, the pigs: fat, pink and enormous! The stys were clean, but the smell was so strong I thought I should die. The sows lay spread out, surrounded by their sucking offspring.

There were horses cantering freely in the field and a little ass, Valentin, had arrived, a present to Reverend Mother.

Of course the whole convent went to see the new arrival. We were allowed to take a walk. Someone made him gallop to the end of the meadow.

We reared rabbits, too, about a hundred of them:

almost an army : they multiplied rapidly. The small ones were fed on condensed milk and rose leaves.

The summer was very hot that year. I was often sent to pick plums with Mother Andrée: a tall professed nun as thin as a rake. We set off together, clogged and hatted, with baskets under our arms. She shook the trees with a stick and I picked up the fruit.

Then came the election of Reverend Mother. Reverend Mother is elected for three years. If she was re-elected three consecutive times by the votes of three-quarters of the community, after the last vote she stayed for six years. Reverend Mother was re-elected and everyone was delighted. The novices were not concerned with such governmental questions. But the ceremony was apparently very moving. All the professed nuns prayed before the voting, which was done in solemn silence.

The second of August was Reverend Mother's feast-day. We had begun to prepare for it as far back as July. Embroidery work was distributed in the novitiate – one towel took days for the most experienced – together with a piece of paper on which everyone wrote down her acts of silence, her sacrifices and the Masses heard for Reverend Mother's intentions. It reminded me of my first Communion . . . In some ways, the Trappistine life is like that of a very strict school.

That month, everyone assumed a grave, mysterious air. On our walks, you could guess that people were carrying skeins of red, green, blue and yellow silk. The work was hidden under their arms. There were secret gatherings in doorways. Then the Mothers separated with a look of careful unconcern. As the great day drew near, the convent took on a festive air. The lay sisters decorated the refectory with ivy. The kitchen smelt of caramel. We went to pick flowers in the garden. At the last moment the Prioress asked me to write something for the novitiate and the externs. I racked my brains. I went through the books in our library. Finally I wrote a little satire for us, a poem for the lay sisters and even a song. Unfortunately the Prioress ordered me to sing it myself. I can't tell you what this act of obedience cost me. So much the worse for their ears. They had asked for it. Mother Josephine, our oldest nun, wrote a long history in verse worthy of Victor Hugo. I was the one who had to read it, alas . . .

The night before, the Prioress asked me to learn the poetry by heart. 'It will be better than reading it,' she said. I learnt it that morning, I recited it in the corridors, I made mistakes, I gabbled it, and grew nervy. I went to the Prioress's office to recite it. I knew it, but I knew it mechanically. I thought about it the whole time. We had an excellent lunch: everyone had fruit, an iced cake, a cup of real coffee and a plate of salad. I looked at my poem between each course.

There was to be a microphone in the workroom, so that our two chaplains, Father Maur and Father Bonaventure, could share in the festivities. The evening before, the novitiate had already offered its good wishes to Reverend Mother in the big parlour. There were flowers in the middle of the room. Under the energetic direction of the Prioress, dressed in our Sunday cloaks, with our acts of silence, our Masses and prayers duly sealed up in an envelope, we had awaited Reverend Mother unflinchingly, drawn up in a row.

. . . . .

My throat was dry. And to think I would have to sing!

My heart was in my boots. How I wished it was over! There were footsteps, and the door opened: there she was! I gave her a bouquet, and kissed her. We sang something. She sat down. Then looked at the envelope, thanked us and chatted to us amicably. The Prioress gave me a sign, and I took the plunge. The poetry went off all right, so did the little comic scene. When it came to the song, I knelt down close beside Reverend Mother and sang in a low voice. I think I turned crimson. There was a distribution of sweets and cakes and a drop of wine. No one said anything. There was a moment's awkwardness, but it quickly vanished. I felt even more like a schoolgirl, sitting there on a bench. Reverend Mother took out her watch. Her duties called her. When she had gone we got up and tidied the room: the preliminary celebrations were over. We brought our work and flowers to Reverend Mother's office, which was transformed for the occasion into something like a stall at a charity bazaar. Things were piled right up to the ceiling. Sister Vincent, a lay sister who usually looked after the garden, had climbed up on a ladder to put plush animals on the top of the cupboard. Mother Emmanuelle had painted a shrine to St. Francis of Assisi. Two of our Japanese convents had sent hand-painted silk scarves, and drawings. There were needlework, pictures, wine, little cups, a bottle with a Bacchus for a stopper! Toys. A bag of sweets sent by an old nun. An amethyst cross. And goodness knows what else!

After lunch, everyone rushed into Reverend Mother's room. This was the official celebration. Everyone knelt before the Mother of the Convent, kissed her, received a holy picture (the lay sisters were very fond of them) and a bar of chocolate. I remember that I ate mine in two days, because I hadn't the right not to eat it. There is a sort of mortification which consists precisely in not mortifying yourself and obeying. Reverend Mother's cheeks were burning after all these kisses, and she was radiant: everyone was delighted. Presently she went off to greet the nuns who were in the infirmary. The whole community went up to Mother Gertrude's workroom; they sang, and played records, and I recited poetry, read Mother Josephine's verse and the little play by the novitiate; it was quite a success, especially with the externs.

When it was all over, we tidied up the workroom, cleared Reverend Mother's desk, and put the flowers in the chapel. The room soon took on its usual appearance: bare walls, empty cupboard, hard bed, and crucifix. I preferred it that way.

II

Illness

EVERY year, in September, the chapter-general of the
Order is held at Cîteaux. The abbés come there from all
over the world. They come from America, Japan, Africa
and Brazil. The Abbé Général presides, and they discuss
the state of each community. Before the meeting, every
monastery makes a Novena to the Holy Spirit. That year
they allowed us another hour's sleep. In consequence, the
walk was cancelled and so was half an hour's working time;
but there was still the same amount of work to be done and
we hurried to wash up after the midday meal. It was no
luxury.

Then came autumn, All Saints' Day, Christmas. My third
Christmas. I counted them lovingly. How many should I
see? Many of them, that I might learn at last to celebrate Thy
coming. Few, that I might join Thee again.

How sweet it was that year, Thy birthday, how rich it
was, what blessings it crowned me with . . .

Ardently I read the prophets who announced Thee. The
words burnt me, came out scorching. 'Unto us a child is
born,' sang the Scripture. Oh, to understand that gift!
There was no one in the chapel that evening, I prostrated
myself full-length on the ground, and I adored Thee.

January was particularly cold that year. The water froze
in the taps. We had to go and find hot water in the showers.
Since I had spent three years in the convent, I thought

myself invulnerable; and, with the consent of the Prioress, I decided to spend a really mortifying Lent. I didn't wear anything woollen and I caught cold. They stuffed me with grog and ordered me to wrap up.

'The true mortification is inside you,' said the Prioress, 'and consists in not doing your own will.'

I obeyed, wrapped up, and drank enough grog to intoxicate myself.

It took me a very long time to throw off that cold. I had such violent migraines that everything was spinning. They made me rest.

'Have you told them how you feel?' asked Father Maur.

'Yes. I can bear our life, but I'm nearly always in a stupor, and when Mother Gertrude makes the slightest remark to me, I feel I could hit her.'

'It's nothing, it's a reaction from fatigue. Haven't they told you to rest?'

'Yes, for a few days, but as soon as I feel better, I'm taking up the Rule again.'

'Yes,' said Father Maur, pensively.

He wasn't at all well himself. He was suffering from a serious heart disease which (as he knew) might take him off at any moment. His voice was getting lower and lower, as if he was stifled. He no longer gave Communion to the eighty enclosed nuns. He was obliged to sit down while Father Bonaventure took his place. On Sunday, during his short and wonderful homily, I looked affectionately at his white face and high cheekbones. Hadn't he given me as a child to God?

'I owe you everything,' I said one evening, when I went to see him.

'I have never felt so ill as I did this afternoon,' he answered.

He never talked about himself. I was astonished, and asked:

'Ill? What do you mean, ill?'

'I had no strength. I couldn't breathe.'

'You must tell them so. Have you seen a doctor?'

The next day, Friday, the day of Confession, he was the same as usual. I listened to him with more attention and respect than I had ever done before. I had a sort of presentiment that I shouldn't be talking to him much longer.

'Father, I love you like a father.'

'You must love only God. God, and God alone.'

'But it is because I love God passionately that I venerate you. You have taught me to love Him. It is said in the Gospel that if you convert a single sinner, you go straight to heaven, and so you will go, if only because of me.'

He laughed. I was electrified by what he said to me then. I asked:

'Is it possible to be as happy as that?'

'You must be thankful, it will not last for ever.'

'It will last always.'

He blessed me.

On Sunday, when he came from the chapel after saying early Mass, he collapsed as he entered the sacristy.

We heard a dull groan and the sound of someone falling to the ground. He was dead. On his feast-day, the fifteenth of January.

The community went to the chapter-house where Reverend Mother told us, with tears in her eyes: 'Father Maur has gone to his eternity.'

We were rooted to the ground.

My first grief at the convent? Was it possible? Yes, the loss of a human being. I shouldn't have thought that friendship could exist in religion. Why hadn't I listened to him better!

His body was laid out in the choir on a bier with candles round it. For twenty-four hours, unceasingly, the sisters came in relays to his side, two by two, reciting psalms. When my turn came, I prayed for my one friend in religion, with all my faith. Lying on the bare wood in his monk's robe, black scapular, white cowl, hollow-cheeked, with God for eternity. 'May he accord me his protection to live and die like him.'

His burial took place in torrential rain. We went in procession to the cemetery reciting the penitential psalms. A funeral isn't sad to us; we sing all the time. It is both a separation and the beginning of an eternal marriage. The clogs slipped and stuck to the ground. The procession advanced only with difficulty. We had to lift our feet – and stamp a little with our heels – hold our cowls close with one hand, an umbrella with the other, and follow the service in the book. Slowly, solemnly, we reached the grave that had been dug overnight. We went down on our knees in the mud to cry three times:

'Lord, have mercy upon Thy sinner!'

Some of the externs were weeping. I controlled myself. On the contrary, I knew I should rejoice. I racked my brains: 'What is it like, this heaven they speak about so often?'

Jean, the monastery workman, and four externs brought up the bier. I looked at Father Maur for the last time. How white he was! His eye-sockets seemed enormous to me. They lowered him straight into the earth, according to the Rule, and censed him. Father Bonaventure blessed the first shovelful of earth. We returned to the convent, singing. Then we took off our sticky clogs and changed our cowls: it was time to go to the refectory.

A few days later our Visiting Father arrived with a

temporary chaplain; we would have to wait a while for the permanent one he had chosen for us.

The Visiting Father gave a eulogy of the dead man. Then he presented our new confessor to us.

Lent was preached by a Franciscan. He was less intellectual than the Dominican of the year before, his piety was more concerned with the physical aspects of the Passion, and turned on a great devotion to the wounds of Christ.

We had a new singing mistress. She was an excellent musician, she taught us the history of the Gregorian chant, and gave us homework to do. We had three or four lessons a week. She was strict even on Sundays. I must admit that the singing grew noticeably better. The reaction of some of the old professed nuns was amusing: they considered that people had always sung as well as they could and that it was a waste of time to try to transform the community into an artistic chorale. But obedience, mother of all the virtues, changed their attitude. What with lessons in Latin, dogma, and catechism, we didn't have a second to spare now for meditation or escaping with God. On Sunday I used to rush, famished, to the chapel, and be transformed into a being living only for adoration. 'If they take this one day from me, I shall kill myself.'

That sacred, blessed, solitary, silent Sunday! I concentrated on it, lost myself, drowned myself in it. 'God, it is good. God, it is a delight. God, it is the only reason for living.'

And then I had to hold out the whole week. Every month, a special Sunday was given up to the most absolute silence. Not a sign. Not one. It was really the castle of the Sleeping Beauty, but all was sleeping for God. Lent seemed very hard to me. My migraines grew worse and lasted the whole day. I felt so sick that when I went out, I had to hold on to the trees so as not to fall. They had sent me out weeding with a little Italian lay sister who signed to me:

'Another ten days and we'll eat.'

On my knees, on the damp earth, I felt faint. I was blue with cold. I thought of little St. Thérèse who had suffered so much without complaint. What a giant, in her way! And even Bernadette. I prayed to them to help me. To let me keep my good humour and hold out. What did you do to hold out when you had reached the end of your strength? Saints, come to my help, I must hold out, I must hold out. I've had enough of it, I can do no more. Help me, Lord. Ah, the bell for the end of work had rung. I should still hold out till the evening. I went slowly towards the novitiate. How I should have liked to sleep!

After Lent, it would be better, wouldn't it? . . . I should try and eat a lot to get well again. It wasn't so long, ten days. Lord, I love Thee.

Besides, the Prioress knew I was tired. She saw it in my face. And then the word 'tired' means so many things! Everyone is 'tired' at the Trappistine convent during Lent. And so much the better, I had come to do penance. God, I love Thee.

My work had been changed: I washed the cream separator in the cheese-dairy, every morning, in two lots of boiling water. In the afternoon I took the cheeses down to the cellar, wiped them and sometimes salted them. I also helped Mother Genevieve to carry the whey to the pigs. The first time I saw those enormous pigs again, I had a nightmare next night and dreamed an enormous pink sow was standing up on its hind legs to devour me.

Mother Genevieve helped me, she was a good companion, though she worried me a good deal. She was the one who taught me how to make cheeses, to shape them as fast as I could and cover them up with linen and a weight so that they dried, and how to wrap up the butter and fold the paper in a certain way. I took a liking to this work, and waited impatiently for the consignments of butter to arrive. I used to get water at the fountain to wash the floor or fill the tubs, it was very heavy to carry. This was much harder than the work in the workroom, and in the end it exhausted me. I didn't realize it at once. I told the Prioress about it, later, but she didn't take me off it.

One of our old lay sisters was dying of cancer in the infirmary. She was admirably patient and brave, and bore atrocious pain without a murmur. I was allowed the honour of looking after her one Sunday. She already looked as if she was not long for this world. I gazed at her intently: at her swollen lips, and drawn features, hollowed by suffering. I prayed that for a few minutes at least she should suffer no more.

Next day, Reverend Mother told the Chapter that she was slightly better. I understood that she was going to die . . . In the afternoon, in the cheese-dairy, we kept looking up at her window. We had lit candles. I saw the silhouettes of the infirmary sister and Reverend Mother.

Mother Genevieve made me a sign:

'She is dead.'

I said joyfully:

'At last, poor woman!'

I saw an expression of terror on Mother Genevieve's face. I was astonished, and said to her:

'She isn't suffering any more, she is with God.'

She was afraid, and answered:

'Who is holy in the eyes of God?'

It seemed to me that death was no longer feared at the convent. The community prayed for your life beyond the

tomb. Death was accepted, awaited, admitted as necessary
to rejoin Him whom one loved. There were moments of
anguish, but joy overcame them since we were all going to
our Father.

.   .   .   .   .

Holy Week began with the usual fervour. On Thursday
evening, with the help of several nuns, Reverend Mother
washed the feet of the whole community in the cloister,
while we chanted the words of Peter to Jesus:
'Thou washest the feet of me, a sinner!'
Some sisters blushed when Reverend Mother washed and
dried their feet. Luckily I always had mine washed by an
assistant.
In the refectory they read the Gospel of St. John.
Still two days to hold out. St. Thérèse, help me!
On Friday, the altar was stripped. The ciborium emptied.
The Blessed Sacrament was at the altar of repose in the
chapter-house. Candles were burning there, and at the foot
of the altar there were sweet-smelling white flowers.
I had been sleeping badly for some time. That night I
heard every hour strike and didn't manage to go to sleep
till eleven. I don't know how I used to get up at all after
such short nights. I used to lie motionless on my bed with
my eyes shut, and try to think about God. Very hard. But
my body still stood up, quite erect, at Matins.
Saturday. At Mass, I noticed that all the lessons in singing
we had endured had borne their fruit: the singing was
lighter, more fluid.
At the Chapter, they read out the tasks: I was the reader
at table. How could I read with this burden of weariness
heavy on my shoulders?

'Give me courage every minute, every second.'

That evening it would be Easter, I should have the strength to do everything since it was Easter. I knew the Exercises by heart, I lived every Office. I had learnt all our customs. At High Mass, I'd heard the reading of all the prophecies predicting Thy coming, Thy sufferings, and the scorn and hate that would be shown Thee. I was full of Thy life, it stuck to my skin, nothing would be able to tear it from me. I was ill, but I had learnt to live according to Thy will.

During lunch, a sunbeam came and coloured the wooden table. It shone with all the colours of the rainbow, then vanished and everything grew dark again.

The hours went by. At the convent we awaited Easter each year with the same faith. Every reading of the Gospels brought new riches. I ran with Peter to the sepulchre; it was open, the linen carefully folded in a corner. He was no longer there.

'Go into Galilee,' said the angel. I ran with Peter.

We retired early to rest. Matins were sung at nine o'clock. We made ourselves beautiful for midnight Mass. I was entrusted with the lighting of the lamps, and I was busy with the harmonium books.

The mother sacristan opened the screen, the altar was lit up. My brother had sent flowers. Father Henry sang Mass.

The usual hot chocolate in the refectory. The choristers were out of breath, and went to rest.

On Sunday, after early Mass, Father Henry spoke to us about the Trinity. He was timid, the paper he held in his hand was trembling a little. We listened to him sympathetically. When the grille of the chapter-house had been shut again, Reverend Mother wished us a good and happy Easter. We bowed in silence.

A bright sun flooded through the novitiate window. No Latin today. I was going to read St. Bernard.

Before lunch, I left the chapel a few minutes before the others, to go and find some books in the chapter-house. I installed myself in the refectory in the reader's chair. I rose when the community came in and bowed as Reverend Mother passed. The nuns advanced slowly, one behind the other: a sight which still moved me after three years.

I asked a blessing from Reverend Mother before I began my reading. I felt so ill I was afraid my voice would fail: no one must notice it. No danger: my voice came out distinctly. I was very close to the microphone. First a passage from the Bible broken off on a sign from Reverend Mother, then the feast of the Saints of the Order, then, finally, the reading book. On a day like this I should have liked to eat my meals with the Sisters. I felt rather exiled high up on that chair.

Lent was over, so there would be two meals a day, that meant two readings: it was just my luck.

They gave me rest, and tonics, and sleeping tablets at night.

Then Reverend Mother came into the novitiate and sent me out into the fields with Mother Aleth and Mother Genevieve. I dragged myself out there. One day, Reverend Mother joined us and hustled Mother Genevieve about in a friendly way. When she had gone, Mother Genevieve signed to me that she was afraid of her. I was so stupefied that I dropped the vegetable I was holding.

'Afraid? Why?'

She laughed:

'I don't know, but I am.'

'Since when?'

'I've always been.'

I added, with the strength of experience:

'You must say some Hail Marys. That's a radical cure.'

'There's nothing to be done about it.'

What an idea! Afraid? I couldn't bring myself to conceive it. Even if Reverend Mother spoke to me drily or harshly, I should find it unpleasant, but I shouldn't be afraid! For me, she was authority. I should do everything she ordered without question, without even thinking, but, apart from that, she didn't *exist*. She commanded, I obeyed. She represented the will of God, but I didn't know who she *was*.

I had come here to seek God and nothing else. The way is that of absolute obedience. I obeyed and I was not concerned with the rest.

Poor Mother Genevieve, who worried me because she was afraid of Reverend Mother! I could have hugged her.

When I came to think about it, I remembered that certain Mothers were afraid of Reverend Mother; that many nuns in the choir missed Office, which was contrary to the strictest rule. St. Benedict demanded the praise of God before everything else. But I didn't want to know anything except God.

In three years, Reverend Mother had only reproached me for one act of forgetfulness. With all my strength I wanted to follow the Rule and live in this intimacy with God.

I had, so to speak, no personal contact with Reverend Mother. Some nuns put a note in her letter-box every Sunday. I marvelled at it. What could they really have to say every Sunday? As for my interviews with the Prioress, I spent them listening to what she told me about her past life. It was always the same thing, but I listened with pleasure. Once, however, when she had asked me what I thought of the externs, I had answered that I didn't care a damn. She rebuked me, reproached me for my freedom of expression and tried hard not to laugh. I prostrated myself and promised her I would correct it in future.

At last a newcomer entered the novitiate: an old nun from Strasburg who was to look after the sick: Sister Jean.

My superiors teased me:

'Sister Bernadette shut the door behind her when she came in.'

'No, no, I didn't shut the door, the proof is that someone else is coming in.'

In spite of the valerian, I was still sleeping badly. I heard nearly every hour in the night as it struck. I began to know those nights in the dormitory. The air blew in fresh gusts through the open window. I saw the sky grow pale, the day break gently. I heard the heavy breathing of my neighbour, the Prioress. 'I don't regret being awake like this, I can pray or just stay with God. Then everything becomes easy, even insomnia.' Just as I was growing drowsy the hour of first rising struck, I still had an hour to sleep, since I was only going to Canonical Matins. The first hour was devoted to prayers, but I had said my prayers all night.

Our temporary chaplain, Father Henry, left us, delighted to go back to his monastery, and on 2 August, Reverend Mother's feast-day, we welcomed not only the Visiting Father, but our new confessor: Father Alphonse.

As Sister Marie-Joseph had fallen ill, the doctor in the little neighbouring town had sent her to be X-rayed at Strasburg. They diagnosed cancer of the intestines. She went into enclosure to be looked after, in fact to die. I knew it through the Prioress. The absolute rest had done her some good. Reverend Mother decided to tell her that she was going to die.

'She's telling her today, after Nones,' whispered the Prioress.

I offered my day for her.

When Reverend Mother went into Sister Marie-Joseph's room, she was just finishing her meal and said, hopefully:

'I'm feeling better, I think that Our Lady must be curing me . . .'

She listened silently to the announcement that she was to die. She wiped her eyes and said:

'It will be as God wishes.'

It was a great grief to Reverend Mother and to all of us. That girl was an angel. We lavished our attentions and prayers on her. She received Extreme Unction in the chapel. She couldn't walk any more, so she was taken into the sacristy in a little carriage. The whole community awaited her, on their knees. I saw her brought back afterwards to the infirmary: dark eyes shining in her pale face.

.   .   .   .   .

She was brought into the big parlour when the novitiate greeted Reverend Mother on her feast-day. I was disgusted. Couldn't they leave her in peace? Was there any use in imposing extra suffering on her? She was dying, but she still had to attend our celebrations. They brought her along in the little carriage, and put her down on the floor, on some blankets. They gave her an injection of morphia; there was a minute little cake and a doll's glass with three drops of wine for her. She smiled. And I, feeling like an imbecile with my stories and poetry, had to recite. I didn't know where to hide myself. Lord, am I going to die, too? I wish I were.

When our greetings and songs were over, Reverend

Mother helped her back to the infirmary. We tidied up the parlour. I went to see the Prioress and told her my internal burnings were so severe that I couldn't stand up any longer, and that I couldn't sleep, in spite of the valerian. I was given stronger sleeping pills and suppositories to ease my pains.

'It's funny,' I thought, 'why aren't they looking after me properly? Is a doctor so expensive?'

When I came out of the Prioress's office, I passed Reverend Mother, I bowed to her. She gave me a charming smile, and I returned it.

It was very hot. Luckily I was working in the cheese cellar. I couldn't bear these summers in the Vosges any more. Continuing my regular life was taking more and more out of me.

And yet the convent garden had never been so beautiful, so full of flowers, so blazing with colours: it was a feast for the eyes. White, mauve, pale yellow, golden gladioli, and irises, nasturtiums, roses and all sorts of little flowers which you don't even suspect the existence of in Paris: they were all growing, blooming and withering. I didn't even know all their names. Yet Sister Marie-Joseph was dying. 'And what about me, was I going to hold out a long time yet? Why weren't they bothering with me? What had I done?'

I said to the Prioress:

'I am exhausted.'

That day, I was received by Reverend Mother. I don't know why I was apprehensive about this interview, but I felt awkward. I had to struggle very hard to remain standing. They overwhelmed me with work which was beyond my strength: instead of helping me to hold out, it seemed that they were trying to exhaust me, and prostrate me. I didn't see why.

No one helped me. I was like the drowning man who was

knocked on the head every time he tried to surface. A few weeks earlier, for the first time, as I came back from the garden, I took another path when I saw Reverend Mother coming. My reaction had been immediate: without reflecting, I had taken a short cut, like a child who had caught sight of a strict headmistress. Why?

I was ready to obey her until death if necessary, but knowing that my death seemed likely to come from her hand, I preferred not to see her. That was all.

I was at the end of my strength; and, since everyone abandoned me, I was going to struggle on alone. Mother Genevieve and the Prioress didn't know about it: they were good companions, but they didn't know. It was a matter between God and me, there were no witnesses.

To think I'd believed I'd become a real nun thanks to a few humiliations and penances according to the Rule! How ridiculous! All that was nothing. Inner sufferings were terrible in quite another way: and all the more terrible because you were alone and you had to be silent.

'Dost Thou not see that I can do no more?' I had said it according to the Rule. What should I do? Nothing. I was happy.

And so, that Thursday, when I'd persuaded myself that everything was all right because I was doing my duty, I went into Reverend Mother's office . . . I knelt according to custom and heard:

'How is Sister Bernadette? We haven't had any news of her for a long time.'

'Mother, all is well, except that I feel very tired.'

She answered drily:

'You will be given rest.'

I had the unpleasant feeling that I had annoyed her. She added:

'You've nothing to say to me?'

Silence. I was thinking.

'No.'

She seemed to reflect, and said:

'The first two years you were perfect, and then for no reason at all you broke with me. You haven't thought of the pain it has given me, the anxiety . . .'

I prostrated myself:

'Mother, what can I say when I am happy?'

She repeated harshly, as if she wanted to hurt me:

'The first two years you were perfect . . . and the third, the third . . .'

I didn't understand, what had I done the third year? I tried to remain standing. If only I could sleep! The bell brought our conversation to an end. I bowed low to her and went out.

I succeeded in holding back my tears until it was time to go to my work. This year which had been so hard, so terribly hard to endure, was a reproach to me. The injustice ought not to hurt me, since I had a clear conscience. The idea of going on alone with such a terrible struggle against suffering and insomnia made me begin to weep again just as Reverend Mother came by. She thought her rebuke had made me weep, and said, laughing:

'And there you are, now, watering your garden. Go in peace. What are you doing?'

'I am going to ask the Prioress for permission to rest.'

She blessed me and went away.

I was in the midst of my trial. I must stay good-humoured. I must not judge. The rest was God's concern.

At night, at least, I no longer needed to move, to stay on my feet, or even move my lips. I looked at Thee. Did I not have the best lot in the world? What should I dare to complain of? Forgive me. I say nothing. 'All is well. All is perfect. And thank Thee for these sleepless nights at Thy side, they are wonderful.' I forced myself to get up. One night, when I felt that this time I COULD NOT, I begged Our Lady:

'Have pity, thou at least. Take me from here or give me the strength to go on. I am indeed ready to die, but if I must die, let me die quickly, if it please thee. I can do no more.'

I went downstairs clutching the banister and struggled to my stall.

I sat there like a corpse and spent my meditation begging for the strength to go down afterwards on my knees. When I had to get up, I collapsed.

12

Dismissal

The Prioress came to pick me up and took me back to my bed. I stayed there all day in a kind of torpor.

Two days later, I managed to go down for a meal. The Prioress asked:

'Do you feel fit to go on as reader?'

I thought: 'She's made of cast iron, doesn't she remember that I fainted the day before yesterday?'

'I will try, Mother.'

I sat up in the chair. The lines grew confused, overlapped each other, my eyes were burning, I couldn't see . . . I read very slowly. I couldn't articulate.

In the almonry, Father Alphonse asked the vestry nun:

'Did they make Sister Bernadette read in spite of her faint?'

They excused me from Matins.

I laughed:

'Whether or not they excuse me, I can't get up any more, anyway.' I found it impossible to sleep at night and I had such burnings that I asked them to call the Prioress.

'Mother, I'm ill, I'm ill . . .'

She was very upset.

'I'm going to tell Reverend Mother about it,' she said. 'Do you want something for your nerves?'

'No, thank you, Mother, there's nothing wrong with my nerves.'

The Visiting Father, who was passing through Épinal, came to pay us a brief visit and asked to see me in the big parlour.

'Good morning, Sister Bernadette. Are you feeling better?'

'Yes, Father, but I still feel tired.'

'The Trappist life is like this.' He drew a straight line in the air. 'And not like this.' He drew a wavy line. 'It mustn't be a trial of strength, it must be continuous. You're young, you have held your own. God doesn't ask you to exhaust your strength.'

I thought: 'Is he going to send me away?'

'You will write to me in a fortnight. Promise?'

'Yes, Father. Must I ask Reverend Mother's permission?'

'No. You know you have the right to write to your Superiors and seal the letter. I'll expect your news in a fortnight, then?'

'Certainly, Father, thank you.'

He blessed me.

I was slightly annoyed to have to write to him. I should look as if I were complaining or being underhand.

Things got no better. I lay on my mattress, in the dormitory, from morning till night. I struggled to get up for early Mass. I went downstairs to sit in the cloister, in the little rose-filled garden. It was delicious there at five in the morning. When the bell sounded for Mass, I went and sat on the invalids' bench. I managed to go to Holy Communion. I came back holding on to the stalls so that I shouldn't stagger. I had become an utter wreck, unable to walk, or stand up, or sleep, or eat: incapable of anything. I had become a mere nothing. And I hardly cared.

After three weeks I was examined by the doctor from C——. The Prioress told him that I was in such a state of exhaustion I couldn't drag myself along any more. He listened to my heart, asked if I was feverish, and prescribed a medicine which soon made me considerably weaker. They made him come a second time, I had slight temperatures, with such violent bouts of sickness that I couldn't swallow a thing. So I went back to the infirmary with the Prioress and the infirmary Mother for another examination. He listened to my heart, felt my liver (it was so swollen you couldn't touch it), ordered calcium injections and asked for tests. He asked me if I was coughing. I think he believed I had consumption.

I was in the dormitory all day. I had tried to go to the cheese-dairy, where the kind Sisters had got the work ready for me and given me a stool to sit on. I was touched by their thoughtfulness. I should so have liked to go on with my work! I kept wondering whether this state would last for long. I didn't go down to the chapel in the mornings any more, but stayed by the rood screen with the aged sisters and Sister Marie-Joseph, who was now walking with a stick. One day she looked at me and smiled. I blew her a kiss. For a moment there was a flash of the old gaiety in her eyes.

And then came my first anguish. A terrible fear took hold of me. Was this dying? How was it going to happen? Would I grow weaker and weaker and disappear? Or what? I called for help: 'I believe, I know, Thou wilt give me strength to bear everything. With Thee, I can do everything, I am not frightened of anything. Let me die, yes, let me die, but don't let me drag on.' I was on my mattress all day. I had a sort of impression that I was being punished, I didn't know what for, that I was not being accepted. I didn't see anyone. No one spoke to me. This would soon have been going on for a fortnight. I had to send my news to Reverend Father. I'd promised. I asked to see the Prioress.

She came to find me and took me into her office. I went straight to the point: the Visiting Father had asked me to write to him.

'I'll give you paper and ink. You can settle down in the novitiate.'

'Thank you, Mother, I should like to tell Reverend Mother. I'm not writing to complain, I'm writing because he asked me to specially.'

'Of course, Sister Bernadette.'

I met Reverend Mother, and said to her, on my knees:

'Reverend Father has asked me to write to him.'

'That's strange, he didn't mention it to me.'

I sealed the letter and gave it to the Prioress.

The sisters I met gave me pitying smiles. I was cut off from the others, I no longer belonged to the convent; I had already ceased to exist. I was plague-stricken.

Reverend Mother fell ill. She had pneumonia again and a temperature of 104°.

On the feast of St. Bernard, the community was allowed a Beethoven concert. I heard it all from my bed. I was so weak that I was delighted not to be at the concert. After Vespers, the Prioress summoned me into her study; or, rather, she came for me and helped me to drag myself there. I thought: 'Goodness, I can still manage to walk, how astonishing! The Prioress has a very strange expression.' She sat down, and pulled up a stool beside her for me to sit on. She looked at me for a long while without saying anything. I waited. Then suddenly:

'Little Sister Bernadette, little Sister Bernadette, you must go.'

'Go? But where?'

She added in a low voice, and as if she regretted it:

'Your health is seriously affected, you must go back into the world.'

Everything swam, I clung to my stool. I felt that I was growing even paler. The Prioress's room was spinning round terribly fast, I had to cling harder and harder. When you get a great blow on the head, you need a little while to react.

I said:

'It isn't possible. I have always obeyed, haven't I? They aren't sending me away for a fault?'

'Little sister, I understand, I do understand.'

She was crying.

'No, it's because of your health. The doctor doesn't know what's wrong with you. He wants you to be looked after outside. He thinks you have a hereditary disease.'

'*Hereditary?* My God! What is it?'

I thought hard. Syphilis? No, impossible. Leucaemia? Cancer? No, if it were cancer, I should have stayed here . . .

The Prioress added:

'I waited till after Vespers so as not to spoil the feast of St. Bernard for you. Reverend Mother wants you to write to your brother: you will be in Paris the day after tomorrow.'

'How is Reverend Mother?'

'Very ill. She finds it hard to breathe.'

She gave me a pen and paper.

The sewing sister came in with my white suit. They were going to wash it, and try it on me.

.   .   .   .   .

It was a grief beyond tears. I felt as if I'd been cut in two.

I must say nothing. Whatever happened, I must say nothing. I must accept. It was the only way to get over it. Yes, perhaps I had made a good entrance, but my exit would hardly be glorious . . . Chucked out for incapacity – and hereditary disease . . . it was Thou that ordained it and Thou knowest how to hurt . . . Anything, but not that: let me suffer, let me not sleep, let me become an outcast, be hungry or cold, anything, anything . . . Anything, I tell Thee, but not that. Don't make me go.

I went to sleep.

Next day the Prioress threw a letter from Boris on to my bed. Boris was a courtesy uncle and I'd sent him a note, nearly a year ago, to ask him to help the Catholics in Vietnam. He was an angel, and he answered that he had done what I asked. I had found him again after all this time. Just the same, affectionate and loyal. Someone warmhearted in this desert. If I go out, he will welcome me, I'm sure of that. But I shan't go out. They will kill me, but I shall stay.

.   .   .   .   .

Before early Mass I went to sit in the cloister, where they had that reproduction of the Holy Shroud. I knew I shouldn't see it again, and I looked at it for a long time to impress the features on my memory. I gazed at the lowered eyelids, the hollow under the bruised eye.

The bell for Mass called me away. I would try and defend myself. But I had grown so weak it was hard to think.

Reverend Mother received me in the morning, she had to go to the clinic that afternoon. She made the effort to see me because I was leaving next day.

Her office was dim. I heard her gasping for breath. I went up to her. The black crucifix was over her bed.

I knelt.

'How are you feeling, Mother?'

She answered with difficulty and a touch of humour:

'We are both doing the will of God.'

She went on slowly, stopping after every word:

'You will take the train for Paris tomorrow.'

'Why Paris, Mother? I don't know where to go. My brother hasn't got a flat. Can't I be looked after near here and come back when I'm cured?'

'What are you afraid of in Paris? God is everywhere. You'll be given the money for the journey.'

'Mother, will you take me back if I get better?'

She hesitated.

'If you are completely cured . . . then . . . we'll see. I think that God wants you to sing His praises . . . in a less austere Order . . . the Benedictines, for instance . . .'

The thought shot through me: I am ill. But what illness is it? They've never said anything in the family. They looked normal . . .

I went on, even though I knew she had finished with me:

'If I am cured, I shan't be able to work in the fields any more, but if I obey submissively . . . I'll do everything I'm told. Mother, you're not sending me away for a fault, it's only because of my health, isn't it?'

'Yes, Sister Bernadette, it's because of your health. You won't recover so quickly.'

She continued, inflexibly:

'You will leave tomorrow.'

She was moved, there were tears in her eyes, she opened her arms to embrace me. I had a second's hesitation, then I let her do so. I bowed deeply while she blessed me for the last time and then I went out.

The Prioress was waiting for me in her office. She hadn't

posted my letter to my brother, because I should arrive before it.

'Reverend Mother insisted on seeing you, in spite of her condition.'

'Mother, could I see Father Alphonse?'

'Yes, in the parlour. I'll ring and take you there.'

Half an hour later, I was talking to him:

'Father, they can't put me out like this. You know they haven't looked after me. They've let me get weaker and weaker. I haven't slept for months. Father, it's impossible for me to go back into the world . . . to Paris . . . I shall die if I do . . .'

'Yes,' said Father Alphonse, 'it's extremely painful to have a nun going back into the world after three years. We don't like it.'

'I haven't gone yet. I still hope. There could be a miracle.'

He smiled. He couldn't do anything. He could only pray for me, and he would pray.

The Prioress came to find me. We avoided speaking. I sank down in her office and said point-blank:

'Mother, I CANNOT take a train all by myself. I shall faint, I know. Let me phone my brother, he'll come and collect me here, it'll only postpone my departure for twenty-four hours.'

I added, smiling:

'You have borne with me for three years, you could surely bear with me another day.'

She reflected a moment and agreed.

I recognized my brother's voice on the phone and felt a moment's happiness:

'Hallo, is that you?'

'Yes . . . Who's that?'

'It's me, Sister Bernadette. Do you recognize me?'

'Of course.'

'Listen, don't worry whatever you do, but I'm very tired. I have to come out to get better. It isn't at all serious. But I'm a bit too groggy all the same to catch the train by myself. Can you come and fetch me?'

'Yes.'

'At once.'

'At once? Wait a bit, I'll ask the editor. Can't I come on Sunday?'

'No, please come at once.'

'All right. I'll take the eight o'clock train tomorrow morning, I shall be there at twelve or one.'

'Thank you. See you tomorrow.'

'See you tomorrow.'

.   .   .   .   .

They tried on my white suit: it almost fitted. They gave me back the few possessions that had been in the attic for three years. They gave me a pair of shoes. The Prioress wanted to give me a pair of silk stockings. I was terrified by such luxury, and took a pair of ankle-socks.

She took me back to the dormitory.

'Don't you want to say good-bye to the novices?'

'Mother, I feel so ill . . .'

She said regretfully:

'As you wish, Sister Bernadette.'

That evening, in the infirmary, they did their best to make me eat, but I couldn't swallow anything. I wanted to die.

I took a double dose of sleeping tablets so that I should sleep and not worry my brother by my appearance.

I felt the curious, pitying looks of the sisters behind the

screen during Mass. Little Sister Marie-Joseph was sitting next to me. How long would she still go on? She smiled at me, but I understood that already she was no longer really with us.

'I've brought you some coffee,' said the Prioress, half opening my bed curtains. 'It's the real thing.'

'Thank you, Mother.'

'Sister Jean will come and wash you.'

'Mother, I can do it myself, if I go slowly.'

'Don't worry, she's used to it.'

I was washed like a baby and I put on my habit again. I still had a few hours to keep it. I fingered it gently. How beautiful it was! And how badly I'd worn it. I thank Thee for all Thou hast given me. I was not good enough to die with Thee. Stop me from judging, stop me from weeping.

The Prioress came to find me:

'Your brother has come.'

'Mother, if you like, I'll say good-bye to the novices.'

Her face lit up. We sat down on a bench, and in came Mother Aleth, Mother Genevieve, Sister Isabelle, Sister Marie-Raymond. They all embraced me.

'We're going to pray for our Sister Bernadette to get well quickly. Aren't we, Sister Bernadette?'

'Mother, I'm going away to take a few extra singing lessons.'

They laughed, said good-bye to me and left to go to Office. I tried not to envy them.

I left the few books I'd been sent in the novitiate. My suitcase was packed. The Prioress gave me a list of what she'd put in. I didn't take in a word she said.

We went to the parlour. In a room close by, I took off our cloak, our serge robe – I felt as if I were being flayed alive – our long billowing chemise, our white stockings and shoes, our veil, our wimple, the band that bound our brows, our coif. I had the head of a little boy. I kissed my cloak and scapular as the Rule demanded.

Without a word, we went to the parlour. The grille opened, my brother was there.

'Hallo, my dear, aren't things all right with you?'

I tried very hard not to cry. The Prioress answered for me: 'She's very tired.'

She left us together.

'Well,' said my brother, 'I've brought you a petticoat, and a skirt from Fath's I've always forgotten to give you . . . I went to see the doctor at C——. He said he didn't know what was wrong with you. But he'd hardly seen you, or tested your heart. But of course, how anyone can test a good sister, through those layers of clothes . . .'

'Not at all, the second time he listened to my heart, and made me cough, it was a proper visit. He's a sort of vet: he doesn't know the first thing.'

I added:

'Don't worry, I'll get better in Paris. I'm glad to see you.'

'We're going back straight away. By the first train.'

'Yes, the Prioress has been very good to me. I'll just say good-bye to her and I'll be with you.'

The Prioress was nearly crying. I didn't want to cry any more.

'Dear Mother, thank you for all you've done for me these last few days. Thank you for your patience with your stupid Sister Bernadette. Can I ask you to pray for me? I hope the novices will forgive me for the bad example I've given them these three years . . .'

Then, bluntly, I asked:

'Mother, what is this hereditary disease you mentioned to me?'

She answered quite directly:

'The doctor isn't sure. He thinks it must be a blood disease, according to the tests.'

'Does he think I'll be cured?'

'Yes, but it'll take a long time.'

'Reverend Mother won't take me back, will she?'

'But of course, Sister Bernadette, if you are completely cured. Now don't think about anything except getting better, that's your only duty.'

'Yes, Mother, so that I can come back. Good-bye, Mother, thank you.'

I went out of the enclosure and joined my brother again.

.   .   .   .   .   .

A few days later the Chapter-general met at Cîteaux, and decided to keep the oblates who had spent at least two years in the convent, whatever the state of their health.

13

A Year of Hope

THE first week I spent in Paris was a martyrdom. My brother installed me in his flat and looked after me with boundless devotion.

The first day, as I woke up, and he brought me my breakfast, I pushed away the steaming cup of coffee and called for Holy Communion. For a moment he was irritated, but he brought round a Father from the Spanish chapel nearby. I could not be deprived of God.

Then I phoned a friend, a doctor. He hadn't forgotten me. He came immediately. He took me to a laboratory, and stayed with me while they took blood tests. Next day he came back with the results:

'What did they treat you for, down there?'

'They weren't quite sure. They gave me sedatives.'

'The idiots! You've been carrying some infection round for five or six months. It was time I stepped in . . .'

'Shall I really get better?'

'Of course.'

'So I can go back to the convent?'

'Don't be in such a hurry. There's some damage. You don't get mended as fast as you fall to bits.'

My brother shared his flat with a friend. I had to move to an hotel. There I fitted up an altar on a little table, and decorated it with roses. The curé of Saint-Honoré brought me Communion.

The rest and the vaccines worked. After five weeks I was better. I wrote to Reverend Mother. When could I go back? The Prioress answered that Reverend Mother was sorry, but there was no question of going back. I was on the point of sending her a pretty downright letter. Far from the Rule, and restored to health, I was no longer resigned to everything. On the contrary, I wanted to fight. Only the thought that it was useless to make a frontal attack stopped me from setting off this epistolary explosion. Instead I wrote to the Visiting Father, who looked after another convent of enclosed nuns, in the Isère. I was brave, I was militant, I had not reached the stage of renouncing a place near God. The affair had hurt me very much, but he wasn't responsible.

The Visiting Father answered that he would do something about me.

I thought I was cured, but I was only in process of being cured. They examined my gall-bladder, watched it, and kept charts. They sent me to Vichy. I was impatient, and they needed every sort of argument to persuade me: if I did not completely recover, my new attempt would be abortive, too. And then what would happen? That argument convinced me. I couldn't allow myself another failure. I didn't possess a soul like Renée's, a soul prepared for a series of rejections. I wanted everything, and at once.

I gave in as regards the cure, but I contrived, at Vichy, to stay with the Franciscan nuns. I was warmly welcomed there. They even offered to let me join the community, the question of health was unimportant. I refused. I was a Trappistine, I would remain a Trappistine.

My brother insisted on coming with me to the cure; but the cure was not so simple. A few days after we arrived, I was stricken with nose-bleeding. My brother was in a fury.

'What sort of state did those sisters get you into, behind their blessed grilles!'

'I was happy there,' I said.

'Happy? Do you know what the doctor said to me? He said you looked as if you had come back from a concentration camp. And you call that the ante-room of heaven! What an extraordinary heaven!'

'Don't hurt me.'

'What would have become of you without Boris and me?'

We spent a week like this. My brother went back. I decided to go and see the Visiting Father.

'I'm so glad to see you,' he said. 'I'm so glad to see you out of that place. The wretches! The wretches!'

I was speechless. He could hardly be speaking about Reverend Mother, and the Prioress?

'They've got asses' heads, just asses' heads, that's all, and their convent is the convent of mediocrity. They aren't contemplative nuns, they are field labourers who think they are contemplatives.'

'Father, you're hard. If I'd had more physical resistance, I should have been happy down there.'

The Franciscan sisters looked after me very well, they almost coddled me. I took my meals in delightful company: a lively old spinster, a teacher of French from Lisbon, and the Mother Superior of a Carmelite convent, who was very pretty and intelligent. Her liver had been ruined by the food in her convent.

My cure was brusquely interrupted. My temperature rose

again. The doctor decided that I must leave Vichy: from time to time (the cases are rare) there are invalids who can't take the cure. I had to leave without seeing the Visiting Father again. I phoned him, and he told me that my one concern, for the moment, must be to recover my health. The Mother Superior of the Carmelite convent said goodbye to me, and said that perhaps, if I wanted, she could welcome me into her community. I thanked her with tears in my eyes. Now that I was unavailable, everyone was claiming me.

My temperature went down and I returned to Paris. Boris invited me, from Brussels, to his son's wedding. I took the plane. I had once known the air hostess, and she was stupefied to see me with a shaved head. 'You've come from the Trappistine convent . . .' she repeated. She could not bring herself to accept it.

Boris was waiting for me at the aerodrome. When he saw me come out of the plane, he gave a start of astonishment as well. He had left a dancer with long hair, and now he found a sort of skinny boy who was awkward in her clothes. I spent two glorious days in his house: it was radiant with the joy of the wedding. But I wasn't used to excitement any more, and everything that concerned my friends and their guests seemed extravagantly futile to me. I wasn't made to live like that any longer.

I went back to l'Allier to meet the Visiting Father; he was still there. I saw the Carmelite Mother Superior again at the Franciscan convent. She repeated her offer to welcome me into her house. She had written to Reverend Mother who had answered with an ambiguous letter, half one thing, half the other, and had made no definite pronouncement on my case. To me it seemed treachery to abandon the Trappistines. I told her so, I said that in any case I was grateful and that I'd enter the Carmelite convent if the Trappistines refused me.

The Visiting Father was waiting for me. As usual he radiated serene benevolence.

'Father,' I said, 'I can join the Carmelites, but it's the Trappistines I want.'

'Very well. You go down to the South of France and have a complete rest. I want you to start your religious life again from zero; I want you to go through the postulancy again, and take your vows. They won't be able to put you out so easily that way . . . Are you ready to begin again?'

'I'm ready for everything, Father.'

I took a taxi to Moulins, a train to Lyons, another train to Nice. My brother was at Menton, and he'd booked a room for me.

I was astonished at the amount of decision I was showing. People who enlist in an organization or an army are supported by a mass of rules and laws. They know what they have to do. They have papers and certificates, they are protected by custom, they can do a certain kind of work which means that they won't become lost property overnight, and they continue to be remotely controlled by the organization which has made them. But nuns are nothing once they have come out of their enclosure. As for me, I might as well have gone to the devil, I could have thrown myself into any enterprise, I had no papers or certificates, and religious authority was no longer exercised over me in any way. I was abandoned.

October, a fine October, is wonderful on the Côte d'Azur. I spent a perfect fortnight at Menton, walking with my brother, or walking alone and serene. At the end of the fortnight, I was summoned by a letter from the Visiting

Father: they expected me at the Trappistine convent in the Isère.

The convent was established in an ancient building, almost a fortress. The chapel had immense vaults, you felt lost in it. The hostel consisted of an icy corridor, three parlours, a first storey with ill-lit rooms, no water, and hardly any furniture. Near the kitchen there was a shop full of medals, statuettes, rosaries, pictures, and missals that were sold to visitors. It was deathly cold.

The Visiting Father introduced himself to the convent confessor, Father Robert, a fine, clear-eyed man, and to the Mother Superior. It was agreed that I must wait patiently for a year before I was enclosed.

I caught a chill, which kept me in bed for a little while. They made me the assistant extern sister, with the privilege of attending Office. Once again joy and confidence were welling up inside me, and I recalled the delights of my first days at U——. I took soothing walks in the forest nearby, with a postulant who was in agony at the thought of being enclosed. I used to reassure her.

This peace was disturbed by an incident (at first I thought it meaningless) about some vases. One cleaning day I noticed two terrible vases, cochineal pink, in the depository where they kept things for the tourists, and their ugliness so maddened me that I threw them into the dustbin. The extern sister wanted to decorate the parlour with them, and looked for them. I didn't want to cause a revolution, so I avoided confessing the truth to her. She turned the whole hostel upside down, grew angry, complained to the Mother Superior and Father Robert. I told the story to Father Bonaventure, the second chaplain, whom I had known in Lorraine (he was Father Robert's assistant), and I asked him to settle things with Father Robert. He told me it was a difficult job, but he'd try to negotiate. I thought they were really making too much of this breakage. The extern sister suspected me without evidence, and cast looks of hatred at me.

One morning Father Robert pushed open the door of the kitchen, where I was, and asked me, fiercely, without preamble:

'And now will you tell me exactly what happened about the vases?'

'Father, I thought they were awful, and I chucked them away.'

'There's no need to talk like a carter. Why did you let the extern sister look for them without telling her anything? You will go and apologize,' said the Father, 'and at once.'

He was no longer a monk. He was an enemy officer interrogating a prisoner. If he'd had a revolver at his side, and a whip in his hand, he could not have looked the part more exactly.

'Father, I'm not used to this tone. You must talk to me more politely.'

Father Robert foamed at the mouth.

'I shall forbid you to enter the convent. You will rot at the door. I know that you are incapable of following the Rule.'

Father Robert was ill himself (he had had an operation), and he had not been following the Rule for months.

'Father, are we responsible for our health?'

'In any case, I shall forbid you to be enclosed until you have apologized to the extern sister.'

He made a theatrical exit, throwing his cape round his shoulders.

The extern sister was good-hearted, and she realized that her complaints had brought an excessive punishment on me. She became attentive, and stuffed me with food. I asked to make a week's retreat to calm my nerves. Afterwards I apologized to the extern sister. Father Robert had now become all honey again, and admitted he'd been brutal, but he said the first virtue of a postulant was docility. I judged from this incident that I had started off worse than I had the first time. This discovery filled me with anxiety. Why didn't God help me any more? Had I disappointed Him?

The winter was severe. I didn't stand up to it. I had to go to bed. The Mother Superior decided that we had been very unwise to arrange my return just before the bad season. She advised me to go away and look after myself, and to come back in June. It was not a dismissal like the time before. All the same, it was a new reminder from heaven. I was being warned.

I went back through Vichy. I was examined again by the doctor who had looked after me during the cure.

'Doctor,' I said to him, 'tell me the truth. Shall I be able to go back to the religious life?'

'You are very delicate. You will hold out three months and collapse again. We will get you right and then it will begin all over again. You are not made for such a hard life.'

In Paris I found my old friend Boris, and my brother, who looked after me with unwearying attention. Boris took me into his beautiful house. I stayed in bed, I couldn't read or write. I followed the funereal procession of hours on the clock. When it was time for Office, I prayed, I saw the Trappistine chapel once again. Christmas wrung my heart. It was a pure festival to me. I had New Year cards: the Visiting Father, the Prioress and the Mother Superior of the Isère were praying for me. They called in another doctor,

because the one who was looking after me didn't seem able
to master my illness: he said I had tachycardia, that I needed
mountain air. They sent me to Austria. I was able to ski a
little. When the snow melted, I went to Rome. I wanted to
be there during Holy Week.

Thanks to a note of recommendation, I stayed at the
Convent of the Assumption, a marble convent, with nuns
in purple, and the triumphant light of the Italian spring
upon it. I plucked up courage, and decided to ask an
audience of the Father General of the Trappists. I was not
risking anything.

A monk with a nice sympathetic look received me,
Father Giovanni: the Father General was travelling. He
listened to the account of my disappointments. He advised
me to go at least once and hear a Benedictine Office,
I should certainly be won over, I was wrong in only
wanting to consider the Trappistines. But I was right and
wrong at the same time, and he could only admire my
obstinacy. He promised me he would give me his full
support.

I visited a great many churches. Everywhere there was
opulence. The Italians do not offer God the same things as
we do: they give their riches, we give our sufferings. In
these sumptuous museums, the memory of the tragedy of
the Passion lost in humanity but gained in majesty. To hear
all the bells of Rome ringing carillons on Easter morning
was to me an unforgettable quarter of an hour. And the
fragile silhouette of the Pope at his window was a touching
sight.

The Mother Superior of the Assumption offered me a
place in her marble convent. I refused. I wasn't free of the
Trappistines. Father Giovanni wrote to the Trappistine
Superior of the Isère and asked for a definite answer,

because it was impossible to keep me waiting; he received a negative reply. I was dragged round in spite of myself in the vortex of the ecclesiastical wilderness of Rome, but it didn't hurt me much: the spectacle of these brilliant bishops, these nuns at ease among the jewels and furs, left me stupefied. The Trappistines hadn't prepared me for anything of the sort.

I left Rome for Florence, where I stayed ten days, going to Communion every morning. When I spoke to my friends about going back to the Trappistines, they didn't contradict me. They behaved as healthy people behave to invalids with obsessions. I was sustained by the constant thought that all was not irremediably finished.

Before I went back to France, I went into retreat in a Trappistine convent in Rome thanks to Father Giovanni. The silence I had regained was a priceless benefit to me. When I came out, after these three days, the Trappistine Superior, in her turn, proposed that I should come back and stay in her convent. She said I could even stay there at once, she would take me as I was, without papers or recommendations. She gave me a room. Three days later, incapable of eating, I left, with the fever consuming me once more. Father Giovanni gave me a lecture: he had carefully advised me not to agree to enter before I'd told him.

When I got to Paris, Boris was there. I told him about my life in Rome and my last attempt.

'You have chosen the finest of careers,' he said to me.

'Yes, but I haven't the strength any more . . .'

.   .   .   .   .

He gave me money. I thought Austria would do me good. And I left for Austria. In a peaceful village with fields and flowers around me, I tried to consider these last months dispassionately. It was like a delirium, the journeys, the comings and goings, the meetings, the doors that had opened and shut again. It was no longer a straight road between God and me, it was a labyrinth.

In November, half rested and calm, I made one more attempt, quite soberly. Just as people who have tried everything in wild passion make an effort to achieve something through wisdom. I chose a convent in the South of France.

.   .   .   .   .   .

I had time. I strolled on the Promenade des Anglais, around the harbour. I no longer knew what I was doing. My stomach felt constricted. Four years ago it had been all right. My adventure had begun again, and today... In all conscience, I was doing what I believed my duty. I had awaited this moment so long I was almost tired by it . . .

The bus stopped. I had some walking to do. The road was up-hill. It was hot.

The South is hospitable, unlike Nancy. A grey-haired man left me as near the convent as he could. The landscape grew wild: terraced fields, and stone; the trees were dried up already. I asked a labourer the way. A path bordered with cypress trees, and a pink roof: that was it.

The colours reassured me a little; at last a convent with some colour about it! I followed the path, it was sandy. I took a short cut through the fields to reach the cypresses. My heart was pounding.

The convent bell, the little hostel, a courtyard, a cemetery. Not a sound. I went in. An old extern sister looked at me with mistrust.

'What do you want, Mademoiselle?'

'To see Reverend Mother, please.'

'Your name?'

I gave it.

A sitting-room, like all the eternal convent sitting-rooms. A table laden with books. Several chairs with their backs against the wall.

The extern sister came back. 'Reverend Mother is waiting for you in the parlour.' Again a table, two chairs, the grille was open. I bowed to her; she smiled. A rubicund face, a big nose not lacking in distinction. Small intelligent eyes behind spectacles. Glacial silence.

'What do you want, Mademoiselle?'

I must be brave. I explained my case and the purpose of my visit.

'What is the name of the convent you've come from?'

'U——'

'You stayed there three years, you say?'

'Yes, Mother.'

'You were sent away just because of your health?'

'Yes.'

'If I accepted you, would you be ready to undergo several medical examinations?'

'Yes, Mother.'

'Why didn't you write?'

'I thought I would rather come and see you. It's hard to explain yourself in a letter. I didn't know you.'

'Mademoiselle, you have caught me unawares. I'm going to write to your convent for information. I'm going to think about it. We don't as a rule like to take a young girl who has left another convent. Have you got a dowry or a trousseau?'

'A trousseau. But if you insist on a dowry, I think my uncle would make some sacrifice for my religious vocation.'

'When did you get here?'

'Only this morning.'

'So you haven't had lunch.'

'. . . No, Mother. Please don't bother anyone. I wanted to see you more than anything else.'

'The extern sister will give you something. You understand, mademoiselle, that I cannot take such a serious decision on the spur of the moment. Would you wait a week? I'll phone the Mother Superior of the Dames du Cénacle, at Cimiez. She'll take you in. They have retreats. Wait there for my answer. I'll go and phone and see you again in a minute.'

She was like Louis XVI disguised as a nun.

She was severe, it was only right. I was cold, and I suddenly felt tired.

The extern sister brought me some lunch, with a smile: there was a bottle of wine, and I certainly needed it.

Louis XVI had chilled me to the heart . . .

. . . But our wonderful life, the silence, Offices, the absolute obedience, and this intimate, permanent contact with God, I should overcome everything to find them again. That three years' happiness, I was ready to suffer everything to find it again. Thy will be done . . . But what was Thy will? . . . I went to the chapel. My emotions and sudden apprehensions, my fears, and rebellion were stilled there, as always. Someone tapped me lightly on the shoulder.

'Reverend Mother is waiting for you . . .'

.   .   .   .   .

'Mademoiselle, I've phoned Cimiez, the Mother Superior will take you in,' said Louis XVI.

'Good-bye, Mother. Thank you.'

She didn't even want to keep me for the night. Where, then, was Cistercian hospitality? It was certainly a bad sign.

I paced up and down and waited for the taxi. I smiled at the extern sister and set off again. The chauffeur didn't wait a minute longer than necessary.

Notre-Dame du Cénacle. A drive leading up to a big white house, an Italianate roof, a garden still full of roses ... The Mother Superior led me to my room, showed me the chapel and dining-room. I dined in company with a variety of women and went up to bed.

There were eight long days to wait . . . But I was following a Trappistine timetable again, and my happiness was almost complete. As there was no retreat at the time, the Mother Superior gave me books and subjects for meditations. Louis XVI was discreet, and had not informed her of my situation.

After a few days, I confided the reason for my stay at Cimiez and my waiting . . .

'Mother, don't you think that Reverend Mother has made her decision? Whatever it is, I do so want to know it.'

'Be patient for another two days.'

Those two days seemed like two centuries.

'Mother, there is no reason for waiting, now . . .'

'Good, I'll go and phone.'

'Thank you, thank you!'

A few minutes later she came back:

'Reverend Mother wants to speak to you.'

I went down like a whirlwind. I opened the door of the phone box.

'Good morning, Mademoiselle.'

'Good morning, Mother.'

'I've been thinking about it. And considering your health, I find it impossible to assume the responsibility. I cannot accept you here.'

'Mother, did you write to my old convent? Did they say something unfavourable?'

'I have had no answer, and that doesn't matter, it doesn't affect my decision. You must understand, Mademoiselle,' she added, 'that I cannot accept you in your state of health.'

'Very well, Mother.'

'I shall pray for you.'

'Thank you, Mother . . .'

I went up to my room again. The Mother Superior guessed. She took my hand, in pity.

'Leave me, Mother, it's nothing.'

She understood and left me. I was holding my tears back very hard. It was no good. My grief was so deep, it had been sustained through so many trials . . . That was my last chance . . . Physically, I couldn't help uttering a sigh of relief. My body could do no more . . . Thou wert right, no doubt . . . Thou wert always right, but it was hard, Thou knewest, to be thrown out like this. I myself had come to love Thee . . . The rest didn't interest me . . . Oh, I don't care a damn, I don't care a bloody damn . . . I beseech Thee, keep me . . . Teach me to be alone with Thee when I am in Paris . . . I am ill, I am ill, I am ill . . .

·   ·   ·   ·   ·

My grief will never be cured. You are not cured of loving God.

The Mother Superior lavished affection and touching attentions on me.

'What are you going to do now?'

'Try and live like everyone else.'

I took the train back to Paris.

I shall always have food for my hunger. I shall never be cold again. My happiness lasted two years and ten months.